Treasured Memories

Treasured Memories

Straight from the Heart

Karen J. Benne

Library of Congress Control Number: 2012914077
ISBN: Softcover   978-1-4771-5357-4
                    Ebook   978-1-4771-5358-1

This book was printed in the United States of America.

To order additional copies of this book, contact:
Xlibris Corporation
1-888-795-4274
www.Xlibris.com
Orders@Xlibris.com
120030

INTRODUCTION

THIS LITTLE BOOK is dedicated to my dad; Theodore Robert Brown, who gave me some of the best times of my life. And filled our lives with some of the fondest memories of the crazy antics he did. He played, he teased, and he was basically just a big kid who had his own (back woods) way about doing things. We call these special techniques "Brown Technology" after his name.

But through it all, we survived. Unlike some children nowadays; we were taught to earn the thing we wanted, and were corrected (without hesitation) when we did wrong. No bribing, no down time, no spoiling, and especially, no talking back. We did what we were told and therefore appreciated everything we had. He taught us the meaning of these words respect, responsibility, and discipline. And above all else, he taught us to obey god, not religion. When I was young, I didn't know all the wheres and what fors; but I can see now, why he did things the way he did.

Even though we had some dysfunctional issues under our roof, I can look back now and have a good laugh. He wasn't a perfect father by no means, but he was my dad, my only dad, and will always hold a special place in my world and in my heart forever. He made our lives interesting. And under our roof, there was never a dull moment. I wrote this for those who never got to know dad, and the kind of person he was. He played like a kid but had the heart of a Lion. I personally am very proud of everything he accomplished, against odds that no one else would have taken. And I know that he touched people's lives in ways that no one else could ever imagine. He was one of a kind. So I hope you enjoy reading about him and how he succeeded in raising all of us kids.

TO GIVE YOU a brief history about the man in question, "my Dad." He was born in Erie, Pennsylvania, July 1, 1930, and From German descendants, who believed in strict behavior and hard work ethics:

And was born with a veil over his face that had to be surgically removed. The veil was a thin piece of skin that completely covered his face. Back then there was a lot of superstitious beliefs. And it was said that anyone born with this veil over their face would have the knowledge to see into the future.

He was also the baby of the family and got by with playing some devious pranks which in turn would get his sister in trouble, in other words, my dad was a "spoiled brat". But when the time came, he would quit school, do his part in supporting his mom by taking on odd jobs working for farmers; taking care of the draft horses was his favorite. He had no father figure to show him or teach him how to grow up and be a man, his dad left when he was very young. So he did not have an easy life.

On October 27, 1947, my dad joined the armed service. With Granma (Anna) Brown's signature, my dad entered the United States' Navy at the tender age of 17.

He would often send money and pictures home from around the world: Brazil, Italy, and the Philippines, just to name a few. To give a description of my dad at that time, he was about 6 ft tall, dark brown wavy hair and weighed in at 146 pounds!

The navy took my dad everywhere; swabbing the deck, all the way. You see, my dad took his (crazy antics) on the ship with him. And although he made it up to a petty officer, when being promoted, he always managed to get knocked back to apprentice seaman. He loved his navy buddies and was always sending pictures of them home. Of yeah! I forgot to mention the ship!

My dad was assigned to the destroyer USS Douglas H. Fox. Little did my dad realize, he would soon become the man that would have made any mother proud. And anyone proud to be his friend and shipmate.

Life on the seas was rough and turbulent. The waters of the Atlantic Ocean could be very unforgiving. There were times my dad would get upset when watching war movies on TV and when I seen he was getting that way, I often wanted to turn the TV off or flip it on to another channel, not realizing it wasn't the movie, but the memories that he had of some of the horror that he went through on the North Atlantic. I don't believe the USS Douglas Fox was involved in any wars during my dad's enlistment, but you don't have to have war to suffer casualties in the armed forces.

When my dad turned 19, his ship hit some turbulent waters south of the Arctic Circle. Waves swept over the bow as freezing cold waters made it difficult for the men on the destroyer to keep their ship on course and equipment intact. Suddenly, without warning, a huge wave came and swept one of my dad's shipmates overboard into the freezing waters of the north Atlantic. Immediately one of these shipmates tied a rope around him and volunteered to try to reach the sailor, but with his hands frozen, could not fasten the rope around his shipmate and was forced to turn back. A cargo net was then thrown over the side of the ship and my dad and another sailor volunteered to go in after the drowning man. With the ship being tossed around like a matchstick, and waves crashing onto the side of the destroyer, tilting it back and forth, my dad and another sailor carefully climbed onto the cargo net (with ropes attached), into the freezing water.

I could only imagine the horror and abuse of the icy cold waters beating the two men against the ship as it rocked back and forth while they hung on for dear life, trying to reach the drowning man.

The other sailor reached out first and hung on to his fellow shipmate but couldn't get the rope tied around him, so my dad swam out and grabbed both of them as they were being tossed around by the rolling waves.

After several rescue attempts, the crew was able to pull the three men aboard. Once aboard the crew had a hard time getting my dad to let go of his shipmates, shock and hypothermia had already affected the frozen sailors.

They risked their lives to save each other: and though they made it out barely alive, the man who was swept overboard was pronounced dead from the extreme temperatures shortly afterwards. As the ship turned back carrying the battered crewman and fallen sailor back to port.

My dad and his fellow shipmate were recommended for the Navy and Marine Corps medal for Heroic Service and Meritorious Conduct in trying to rescue another sailor from the freezing waters of the North Atlantic and were awarded the honor after their ship came into dock.

While the other sailors went home on shore leave visiting their families, my dad was sent to a naval hospital in South Carolina. Little did he know, he would never see his ship or shipmates again.

My dad suffered physical and mental scars from the rescue attempt. The freezing waters left him needing weeks of physical therapy and he suffered from terrible nightmares every night. He would often cry out "Man Overboard" and thrash around in a swimming motion in his sleep. He often dreamed of his shipmates' heads bobbing in the water and him trying to save them. These nightmares would be there to haunt him throughout his life. While he was at the hospital, he wrote home to his mom and to his girl; who was patiently waiting for him. I'm sure he was wondering what was going to happen: would he still have a career in the navy; or would he be sent home?

On April 7, 1950, my dad was given an honorable discharge from the navy. He received a $1,000.00 settlement and about $123.00 worth of pay and travel expenses and was sent home.

It was a good career while it lasted. The Navy took dad all around the world. He made friends, and lost friends. He sent souvenirs home from Italy, the Philippines, Belgium, and all the provinces along the North Atlantic. Anywhere his Ship would dock, he was always thinking of his mom and his girl. He sent home teapots, dishes, salt and peppershakers, foreign money, and pictures of him and his shipmates. But now he was at the crossroads and he knew the direction he had to take. It was time to leave the past behind and start thinking about his future.

Now that Dad's navy days were over, he could look forward to a new life, getting a job and making a home for his "bride to be" was often on his mind. My dad had her name tattooed on various parts of his body when he was in the Navy. Each finger had the letters in her name on them, and her initials on his legs along with the navy eagle tattooed on his forearm. They were symbols of his love for her and his country.

After returning home, Dad started a new job operating heavy equipment for a local landscaper. Wedding plans were soon in order. Dad bought a small 20-foot trailer for them to live in, and on May 29, a marriage certificate and blood tests were sought out. His mom would sign it for him, and her dad would sign for her: and on June 8, 1950 the two were married in a local chapel with a small group of friends and relatives looking on. They spent their honeymoon in their cozy home, which was in the city suburb, located not far from the local grocer, an elementary school, and his in-laws. This would be temporary until a house was built.

My dad was a hard worker. I have many pictures of my dad and Grandpa either setting concrete blocks, or digging with picks and shovels. He often would go to Grandpa and Grandma's to help out. He was a good son-in-law and they loved him dearly.

I don't know how long they lived in the trailer. The winters would have been too harsh (I would have imagined) for them to have lived in there for very long. But with the help of family and friends, a house would soon be in the works. I'm sure the landscaping job dad had would soon pay off. Eventually a lot was cleared and the process of digging a basement and purchasing the blocks was in the process. It would be a small 1-bedroom 1-bath house with a full basement and formal dining room separate from the eat-in kitchen. And really a nice home for the couple to raise a family. The basement had an area for kids to play, a workshop for him and a nice area for the ringer-washer and plenty of space for clothes to hang and dry in the wintertime. On the main floor I can remember the pink floral linoleum floor covering throughout the house along with the white metal cabinets and a white with black trim porcelain top metal table with a small drawer built in it in the kitchen. Mom would put decals of swans on the bathroom cabinets and had some Aunt Jemima kitchen decor and a collection of salt and peppershakers. In the basement stairway was where my dad would hang his hunting rifles: he was an outdoorsman and would often share his harvest with his friends and family.

As a child I always thought we had a pretty big yard, (but when you're a kid, everything looks big). There was a combination shed-dog coop in the back yard and later on a vegetable garden (where mom grew rhubarb) and swing set would be added soon and they would be expecting their first child. And on April 1, 1953, my sister was born.

Dad was a good provider. He was always doing something for someone or working around the house. One morning he came home with his hand wrapped up and his arm in a cast. Apparently (when he was working at the plating company) he was operating a buffing machine and it grabbed him and pulled him into it. He wound up having to get plates in his arm because the machine crushed it and cut off two of dad's fingers on his left hand. He was off work for awhile I imagine, but it didn't slow him down. He was tough and wasn't going to let a couple less fingers slow him down.

With a wife and child to support, dad took a job working nights for a plating company. It wasn't unusual for dad to take on more than one job. He was a get-r-done type guy and the skills he learned in the Navy and the knowledge it took to build their house would come in handy for earning extra income.

Soon the neighborhood was growing. There would be sidewalks being poured and things were looking up. New homes were being built on the block and new businesses were on the rise. And the little house would soon have extra 2 bedrooms added on in the back. Mom and Dad's bedroom had a nice double bed with matching dressers and a large closet to hang clothes in and keep mom's cedar chest in. She would always hide the home made Christmas cookies in the chest along with a special place for Dad's navy uniform and other things she cherished. Mom was meticulous about her housekeeping. The outside of the house had tar-paper on it; but after the addition was added on, Dad put the insulated brick patterned tar paper siding on and the house was looking a bit more complete. In the meantime the little trailer that was their first home would be sold to one of my uncles and was moved up to the mountains and used periodically for a hunting camper; where my dad and uncle would go hunting together.

Life in the 50s was good for the young couple and it wouldn't be long until another child would be born.

On February 8, 1956 Karen Jean Brown would be coming home for the first time. I guess I was an unexpected child and Mom had some difficulty adapting and I spent some time with Grandma until mom was ready to take care of me. But once she got me back, she couldn't let me go and loved my sister and I as a mom should. She took very good care of us at all times. Now that the family was complete, Carol and I had it made, we had our aunts and uncles and grandparents only a few blocks away and plenty of kids to play with. All of us kids had a run of the neighborhood. Mom would call our names and we would come running home or we would come home riding our bikes down the road without our hands on the handlebars. It's a wonder we didn't wreck our bikes. The street we lived on was a dirt road with oil or tar sprayed on it to control the dust. Mom always had to wash this tarry stuff out of our clothes. I remember one time the city just got done spraying the road, and I was always going in and out of the house, well Mom was getting tired of having to clean the tar off of my shoes so she told me to take them off; I did. And the next thing I knew she was running out of the house and picking me up and carrying me back in the house; I guess she didn't want me out in the tar in my stocking feet either. Back then parents should have been more specific. But growing up in our area was fun.

We had a few pets too; Dad had his hunting dogs, 2 beagles. One was black, white and brown. Her name was Sassy and the other one's name was Snicklefritz, she was a darker colored (what they called Blue Tick) hound. Being both beagles, they were rabbit hunting champions.

Dad would bring back enough rabbits to supply the whole neighborhood. We also had a dog named Ernie. He was a big dog that was part Chow and part Saint Bernard. We would hook Ernie up to a sled in the wintertime and he would pull us around all over. He never hurt any of us kids, but one day Ernie, being such a big dog, accidentally knocked one of the neighborhood kids down and Dad had to resort to then tying him up. He didn't take to being tied up very well and would often jump out at the end of his chain and would scare kids in the neighborhood. I'll never forget how hurt dad was when he came home and found Ernie with blood all over his face because some bad kids were poking the dog in the face with sticks. Ernie was nearly blind. He had blood coming from his eyes and Dad had to take him away and came home without him. He was Dad's dog and it upset him to have to put him down. We loved Ernie and it was sad for a while having to live without him; especially when there were two small children that couldn't understand what had just happened.

We had some other pets too: Donald was a female duck who was always pestering mom every time she went outside to hang her laundry up on the clothes line. Mom would turn her back to hang something up and Donald would be in her laundry basket. Next thing we knew, she was chasing the duck all around the yard. Donald was a big white duck and pretty much ruled the yard. She would stalk my mom to get at that basket full of cold wet clothes. Mom would yell and the duck would "Quack, quack, quack" back at her. We also had a white rabbit name "Uncle Pete". It seemed odd that Uncle Pete's cage was on the other side of the shed. This is the same shed the dog kennels were attached to. But it was a nice cage. He could get in and out of the weather. I think Uncle Pete was in the house a few times but I don't quite remember for sure. Our swing set was in the back yard area. I remember my sister hanging upside down, falling off the swing set, and breaking her elbow. She had a half cast she had to wear for a while. We would often be playing on the swings, watching mom hang up clothes.

We also had a chicken named "Henrietta". My dad went to help someone butcher chickens one day and made the mistake of taking my sister with him. She got upset and clung on to one of the chickens and wouldn't let dad have her. So while my sister was crying my dad gave in and Carol came home with a chicken in a bag! The chicken and duck were good buddies. But sometimes Henrietta would fly up on our heads. Although we didn't mind it, Mom had a hard time trying to hang clothes out on the line with a chicken wanting to land on her head and a duck shagging her around the yard to get at the laundry basket. But mom was a good sport about it and let us kids have our pets.

My sister and I each had our own bedrooms. I can remember having "Snow White and the Seven Dwarves" decorations on my bedroom walls and a nice closet to hang my clothes and put my toys in. We had hobbies too" we had the paint-by-number kits, board games with moving parts, and a loom set to make potholders out of. My sister and dad would put their own models together. Dad had a model of a destroyer he put together. It was gray in color with all kinds of neat guns and little stuff on it. We kids knew better than to mess with it. We walked the straight and narrow because if we didn't then Dad would spank our butts. He was often complimented on how well-behaved Carol and I were when he took us anywhere. That's because he would put the fear of God in us, so we knew if we behaved we would get to go anywhere with Dad.

Sometimes Dad would get his harmonica out and entertain us with some old tunes. He used to bounce me on his knee and he wrote a song about me called "Itty Bitty Bump Bumps". He always sang it to me. That's when I got the nickname "Itty". My first nickname was "worm". I'm glad that one didn't stick but "Itty" and "Sis" did. At around this time Dad would take on another job, in addition to his shop job. He took on a job, what we would call, "Rent-a-Cop". He wasn't working too much for the excavation business anymore and felt it was time to take on another part time job. He had to go through a training course and do a lot of book studying about where the pressure points were in a person's body for self-defense, and some kind of other tactical defense movements. He would be studying all the time. My sister would sometimes bug him when he was studying, but he would pass his tests and get a job working for the Erie Crawford County Police Department. His uniform would look very similar to the police officer uniforms and he would carry his 38 pistol with him. He would often be hired to patrol places like the speedways and county fairs, etc. He would often take Carol and I to the speedway with him. I don't think the Erie Police Force liked the "Rent-a-Cops" though, because it replaced the jobs of the full time policemen. But Dad didn't care and could be anywhere they needed him.

He would always take my sister and I with him everywhere. We would go to the Warner theater in Erie and see all the Walt Disney movies like "Snow White", "Old Yeller", "Sinbad the Sailor", Bambi", and of course all of the "Godzilla" movies. He'd take mom and Carol and I to the drive-in too. We loved going to the drive-in and playing at the playground in front of the big screen. When it got dark we would hurry up and get back to our car in time to watch the movie. I remember Dad paying the person in the little pay booth and driving around looking for the speaker that worked. During intermission we could peek in where the projectors were and see how they worked. There were always two projectors that had to be in sync with each other so when one ran out, the other had to continue on with no glitches, so the audience would never know. Everything had to be precise. I can still smell the food. The hamburgers were so good. We loved the intermission too, so we could go back out and play on the playground or go the snack bar.

The T.V. Shows were cool too. I remember watching the "Mickey Mouse Club", "Howdy Doody", "Captain Kangaroo", and the original "Batman" with Adam West and Burt Ward. The "Monkees" was my favorite show or maybe it was the Captain with his magic drawing board, Mr. Green Jeans, Mr. Moose and Bunny Rabbit. We had our favorite cartons we watched too, like "The Bugs Bunny and Road Runner show", and all the Hanna-Barbara cartoons like "Yogi Bear and Huckleberry Hound". The commercials in the wintertime around Christmas time were cool too. There were the three clay-mation elves called "Hardrock, Cocoa", and "Joe". Along with that would be the "Suzy Snowflake" one that my sister and I still know some of the words to. Also there were the Norelco floating heads elves that would come sleighing down a hill on an electric razor. There was another program using puppets called "Fireball X-L 5, that I just loved to watch. It was about these puppet pilots who saved the world in their space ship called the Fireball X-L 5. It was so neat. These were just some of our favorites. I couldn't forget the horse programs like "Mr. Ed" and "My Friend Flicka."

We had an RCA television with rabbit ear antenna on it. There was no color TV or remote control back then. We kids were the remote control. Mom had a rocking chair she would sit in and if one of us rocked the chair without sitting in it, she would freak out because she was superstitious. We couldn't open our umbrella in the house either. It may have been because mom was part Cherokee Indian. Mom was a very pretty woman. She had very dark wavy hair and hazel colored eyes. She always gave me back rubs and made us lemon meringue pies!

Soon it was time to remodel the kitchen. My sister and I were both in school now, so dad had our neighbor, who had a cabinet shop in the neighborhood, make mom some new kitchen cabinets. The earlier old porcelain table was replaced with a gray Formica table with chrome legs. It was much bigger and could accommodate our little family by giving us more room for sitting. Mom was happy with the new look and added her own little touches.

My sister's room was neat too. She had monster models that she put together and painted. Those were so cool. I would always go in her room and look at them. She had Frankenstein, Wolfman, Phantom of the Opera, the Hunchback of Notre Dame, the Mummy and even the Munster Mobile. I believe she had them all, even Dracula. She had this horse series collection, too. There was a lot of stuff, like her guitar that she took lessons on. She had our pet salamanders in an aquarium that Dad would bring back from Chapman's Dam for us. I had some neat stuff, too. Mom hung Snow White and the Seven Dwarves up all around my room. I had all my stuffed animals on my bed that I slept with because I was scared of the dark. The city lights would always cast a shadow through the trees at night and when the wind blew, they would wave back and forth and scare me. Sometimes I would crawl in bed with Mom since Dad was at work.

With Dad being at work nights and Mom being at home, my sister and I seemed to be having a pretty good childhood thus far. Occasionally we would go to grandma and grandpa's for family picnics. My aunts, uncles and cousins were there and we always had fun running around and playing. My great Grandpa Ed always sat at one end of the table and Grandpa Lynn would sit at the other end. Picnic time was fun: my mom had two brothers and two sisters. It was nice having her family close by. My dad's mom and siblings lived in the city, too, and we would often go visit my dad's neices, nephews and my aunts and uncles on his side of the family. He had one brother and four sisters. They didn't have any kids our age to play with since Dad was the baby of the family. All of their kids were much older than my sister and I.

One time when we were at my mom's family's picnic, my cousins had a big boxer named Ginger. We kids were all playing fetch with her. She could jump up and take the stick out of the big kid's hands. Well, I decided to grab the stick and hold it up and Ginger mistook my skinny little arm for the stick and snapped my arm like a twig. Needless to say, playtime was over and off to the hospital I went. I wound up with a full cast on my arm. I hated that cast; it was so itchy that Dad made me a scratching stick to shove down in there to help control the itching. I was glad when I could finally get rid of it. My sister and I often would go to Vacation Bible School in the summer months. I remember the Kool-Aid and cookie combinations they gave us there. It was not a good combo. The cookies made the Kool-Aid tart, but I guess that was all the little community had for us. Whenever I go back home we'd drive past Belle Valley and still see the building there.

I remember a time when I had to take mint-flavored cod liver oil. Now there's an experience I don't wish on anyone. I guess Dad and Mom had to take me to the doctor because I wouldn't eat anything. The doctor's name was Vitanza, and he instructed them to give me that crap. But for some odd reason I don't think I complained too much. I don't think my sister appreciated it though. She described me as a skinny, frail, little kid with baby doll hair and fishy smelling breath that would follow her around everywhere. She and her friend would always try to get rid of me. I know of a time when my sister locked me in the dog shed and she and her friend took my bike and went bike riding in the neighborhood. I don't know how long I was in there with the dogs and rabbit but I remember panicking and breaking the window out in the shed and I cut my hand a little on the glass. My sister got a spanking, and I had to have a double shot of the ol' cod liver oil after that. Back then it was a miracle cure for just about everything. Mom kept it in the refrigerator door next to the catsup. It's a wonder the neighborhood cats didn't chase me around.

They would take us to the dentist, too. We had a black dentist named Dr. Barret. Dad took me there one time to have one of my molars pulled. It was a baby tooth that was rotten and had gotten infected. I don't guess there was any Novocain back then because I don't remember anything being pain free. That dentist put me in that chair, and started pulling that tooth out. I can still remember the pain. I dug my fingernails into the wooden armrests of that chair. I didn't like him, and I don't think Carol liked him either, because she bit the crap outta him once. He probably deserved it. Once was enough for me. I made sure I brushed my teeth after that.

When you were a little kid did you ever want to crack rocks on the sidewalk? I loved cracking rocks. I would go down in the basement in Dad's workshop area and get one of his hammers and break stones all day. I liked the pink ones with the black and white sparkles in them and also the black and white striped ones with sparkled crystals in them. I liked rocks; even today I'm always looking at them. I know which ones have the crystals in them to this day. Not that I'm an expert on rocks or anything. Another thing we did as a kid is we always played hopscotch. Every sidewalk in the neighborhood had colored chalk on it in the form of the hopscotch game. Our sidewalk in front of our house had a downhill slant on it, and after I learned how to ride a two-wheeler bike, I got a skateboard and would sail down the sidewalk in front of the house. But I had to think fast and jump off before the sidewalk ended; or I'd go flying somewhere on my butt.

We had burn barrels and trashcans back then and the garbage man had to dump those big 50 gallon trashcans of garbage into the trucks. I remember dad invited the garbage man in the house one time. He was a tall thin black man. I don't think I ever had seen him close up before or perhaps just didn't pay much attention, but I clearly remember checking him out, (you know how little kids tend to stare) and saying something like, "You have chocolate hands." He'd say, "Yes, I do" and he'd smile. Then I'd say, "You got chocolate arms." He'd react with a surprised look on his face, and say "Why, I have at that," as he looked on in a shocked and amazed way. Then I couldn't help but say next, "Why you're chocolate all over!" Then he gave out a big laugh. I liked our trash man; he was a nice guy.

I had a best friend back then, too. Her name was Lou Ann. She was a red-haired girl that lived a few doors down. We went everywhere together. Our moms were friends and we were always at each other's houses. She had a Barbie doll and I had a Midge doll. We'd exchange doll clothes and play her Twister game all the time. Her dad played the accordion and was always practicing in the next room for the Polka band he was in. We rode our bikes around and played hopscotch, red rover and jumped rope, and even mastered double Dutch. She was my comrade. We played together and got in trouble together. With the neighborhood expanding there was always something to get into. We had a neighbor named Bert who lived behind us. He had a Harley and once gave us kids a ride on it. He also had a huge swing in his back yard that we couldn't stay off of. It was big enough to accommodate the whole neighborhood. We would all pile on it and two of us would push it and then run under it. Bert was always chasing us out of his yard but we would always come back because of his swing. I remember when the house next to ours was being built; we were always playing in the dirt. I had a lot of trucks and cars and a farm set that I'd play with. I was a tomboy. I really didn't care for dolls and such. I loved Tonka toys and making mud pies. There was a boy named Kevin who used to come over once in awhile. His house had the biggest sandbox ever. We would play over there once in awhile, until the neighborhood cats starting using it for a big litter box. When the house was going up next door, Lou Ann and I would be playing in the dirt making mud pies and goofy Kevin came over one day. Lou Ann and I didn't want him around us at the time, so I talked him into eating one of the mud pies we had made. I couldn't believe he actually took a bite into one. After that he cried and went home. I don't remember seeing too much of him after that. Once the house was built, our new neighbors moved in. They had two kids, named Chris and Levi. Levi was mentally challenged. While Lou Ann and Chris were off at communion, I would go over and play with Levi. I pretended to be a schoolteacher and he was my student. It was a little hard to understand him sometimes, but that was okay. He was a lot younger than I was and with a handicap his mom didn't let him get out too much without supervision, so we played in their basement a lot. Lou Ann and I liked collecting rocks. I didn't know what a rock garden was. One day Dad came home and couldn't get the dresser drawer down in the playroom in the basement open. He tugged and tugged thinking it was stuck. Well it wasn't stuck; it was full of rocks that Lou Ann and I stole from the neighbor's flowerbed. I remember mom standing at the door making Lou Ann and I put the rocks back. My sister said Mom held the screen door open and pointed her finger at the neighbor's rock garden, (at the side of their house) and made sure we brought all those rocks from the basement back where they came from.

I tried to stay out of trouble and be a good kid, I didn't want to be bad. When I was good, Mom would give me ten cents to buy some penny candy at the local store. The wax lips, pixie stix and candy lipstick were my favorites.

After that episode, I think I turned my attention to the train sets my dad had set up for my sister and I in the playroom down in the basement. Carol had an Amtrak passenger train and mine was the locomotive with a coal car. He rigged up two tracks on some plywood and made little trees and grass, and I think there was tunnel, but I'm not sure. I would be down there playing for hours. My locomotive came with a bottle of oil. When you put a drop of oil in its short smoke stack, it would start puffing smoke as it ran around the track. Dad would come down and play with them with us. He tried to spend as much time with Carol and I as he could. He was still working at the plating shop and probably still helping out the landscaper, (whose name was Andy), at that time. My dad did other stuff with us. Once he got this old army tent and we would run and get in it so we could get in and out when it rained. The tent was moldy smelling and the roof leaked. It would start dripping if you poked at the roof from the inside, so Dad would wait till it would start pouring down rain, and then he'd poke the tent above where we were standing and it would start dripping on us. But we had a place that we could run in and out and get all sloppy. We had a shed for our shoes so Mom wouldn't have to worry about keeping the floor clean.

When school was in session we could walk to school, and even come home for lunch. My typical school day would start out with me getting all my stuffed animals and myself out of bed. I would go to my closet and pick out the dress or jumper. (Mom and Dad would let us pick out our own stuff.) Then I would get into my dresser drawer and pick out one pair of the many assorted colors of leotards that I often wore. I had the regular stretchy kind or the thicker wooly ones for when it got cooler out. Boy did it ever get cold out, especially in the wintertime. But I don't think we thought too much about the cold and snow because we always had some other type of activity we did outside. All of us kids would gather up and go to this vacant lot we knew about that had a perfect hill for sledding down. It was just before Grandma and Grandpa's house on the opposite side of the street. If we needed to take a break from a hard day of sledding, we could go to our gram and gramp's house and visit them and warm up at the same time.

Dad would grab a snow shovel after removing the snow from our driveway and he would make a snow fort or an igloo out in the yard. We would all go out and play in there all the time in the winter. It was fun building snowmen too. We always had a snowman in the yard somewhere surrounded by snow angels.

My mom had a parakeet named Dicky. He was a pretty little bird, turquoise in color, and his cage door was always left open so he could come out and fly around whenever he wanted. He would chirp and jabber all the time. Mom would teach him to talk. He always said, "Dicky bird, pretty bird, pretty bird." He was always letting us know he was around. He'd fly and land on People's heads or on their shoulders. He would flutter around and hang upside down on the curtains. I remember when he was out once, he kept flying in a book I was looking at. I don't know what possessed me to do it, but I attempted to close that little bird up in that book. I gave him a flying chance so I was slow about it, thank God, or Mom would have had a heart attack. I think after that "Dicky Bird" didn't have as much run of the place as he wanted. He would squawk as loud as he could and have a fit so Mom would cover up his cage to keep him a little quiet at times. Poor bird, it was all my fault. I think he got to be out all day while I was at school though.

Dad would often take us to an amusement park called Waldameer. As soon as we walked in they had a penny arcade with all kinds of neat old mechanical picture show type movie cards (flipping things) that I would run to and drop my penny into and watch the cards flipping fast enough to watch a girl dancing or a car racing. I wish I knew what the name of those things were. After the penny arcade was the "Dodgem' Bumper Cars". Dad would always put me in with him, I was a bit squished, but I never complained. After that we would get on the "Comet". It was the coolest roller coaster ever, (and the oldest). It was all wood. When we got on it you could just smell the antiqueness of it and hear the boards clitter clatter as it made its way up the incline and when it got to the top it would wind and turned down the rickety railway. It was fast and fun. Then we would always make it over to the Tilt-a-Whirl and Dad would sit on the end. When it whirled around he'd slide over and squash us. They had boat rides and the "Thunder River Plume Ride". Dad would always put my sister and I where we would come out soaked. The antique merry-go-round was the neatest ever. It had dragons, ostriches, lions, tigers, and of course, the colorfully decorated horses all carved from wood. The sights and smells, cotton candy and games were so much fun. Believe it or not Waldameer made it in history as having one of the oldest working roller coasters in the world to this day. I'm going on 54 years old and when I go up and see my sister I always make a day of going to Waldameer just for old time's sake. But I'm getting a little too far ahead, so let's go back to the 60's.

I guess as you can tell, my dad cherished my sister and I. He was a lot of fun. I don't remember mom going with us too much, even when it came to grocery shopping. Mom would go with Dad to pick up the check at the Plating Shop, (because he was still working nights), and she would be there when we picked Grandma Brown up and went for rides out in the country to watch the leaves turning in the fall; but mostly it was Dad and us. I asked my sister about this and from what I gathered from our conversation Mom was a very meticulous person. When Mom and Dad were dating things seemed to be pretty normal. They would hug and cuddle like any other couple in love. Things seemed okay when Dad would come home on leave from the Navy. But when Dad got home from the Navy, (as I wrote earlier in this book), he wasn't the same man. He was a good provider but something was missing in their relationship. Since my sister and I were still too young to know any difference, we never saw anything coming. You see Mom stayed at home all the time. She kept the house very clean and I think she was a "Keep up with the Jones" type person who did her womanly chores and was always watching soap operas on TV. She always had her makeup on, kept her hair nice and was a meticulous but very vain individual. Where Dad on the other hand wore his dirty shop clothes everywhere and when it came to money matters he made sure he was in total control. Plus back then if you had any kind of deformity, (like his arm and fingers being mutilated in the machine where he worked), a person was considered a freak. I can only imagine the strain on the marriage. Plus with Mom watching soap operas all day and Dad working nights, I can only imagine that something was going to go sour. They wouldn't be sleeping together and Mom would want to be romanced and Dad was always working. Plus I'm not sure that Dad really knew how to treat a woman because he had no father figure to learn from. So it was no wonder a divorce was going to be inevitable. I remember Dad saying how Mom was never satisfied. I think she had needs that Dad wasn't there to give her; my dad, being the sole supporter and things having to be done his way; well let's just say we can't point a finger at just one. I think my Mom's mom (Grandma) may have tended to meddle just a little too, but I can't swear to it. I think Mom wanted to be wined and dined and Dad didn't turn out to be the "lovey-dovey" type. So my mom and dad separated and Dad took up residence with a woman named Ruby and six of her children. Mom started dating my uncle. Yeah, you read it right. It seemed like a train wreck waiting to happen. Well, my uncle was married to my mom's sister. I can only assume that my aunt and uncle were already divorced. Ruby and her husband were already divorced, leaving her with six kids. My uncle was very good, at that time to Carol and I. I was about eight years old at the time and Carol was about eleven and no one seemed to be upset about this arrangement. But my ex-uncle soon to be step-dad had his children that he didn't seem to want too much to do with. My aunt and cousins all lived with Granma and Grampa at their house. Now personally, as I looked back, I could not imagine dating my sister's husband, (divorced or not). But I guess as long as it was all kept in the family that perhaps that made it okay. What made it even more ironic was the fact that his last name was also Brown, (No relation to my dad, thank God). Now my dad and Ruby's kids lived in a small apartment in Erie in one of the worst parts of town, living in poverty. Every time my sister and I would spend the weekends over there we would see the downstairs neighbor's children running around filthy and naked. This putrid smell came from their apartment and we wondered if perhaps they didn't have any running water to clean up with. Staying upstairs with these other kids who were strangers to us was a circus, and I'm not talking about the ones Dad took us to either. We had to sleep three in a bed, which I hated because someone's knee was always in my back. Carol and I would always get lice in our hair and bit up by bedbugs. Every time we would go back home to Mom the school would send Carol and I home and Mom would have to scrub us down and run that steel comb through our hair. It was awful. Then to see my dad giving all his attention to these other kids and not giving Carol and I any attention was an adjustment I wasn't sure we could handle. But my dad lived with her, (Ruby), for a year. I was always wanting to go back home and sometimes Dad would take me back home to Mom and Uncle Ron, (Red). I remember how I especially hated the sleeping arrangements. I was used to sleeping by myself in my big bed at home with my stuffed animals and not with two other kids whose legs and knees were all over me. I would practically have to beat the crap out of them just to get them away from me. So I never got any sleep on the weekends I stayed over there.

There was one time Dad got his butt chewed out really bad by Mom. I came home with one less tooth in my head. We were playing "Blind Man's Bluff", and I happened to be the blind man with a blindfold on. I was too little to know the rules of the game, and I started jumping up and down on a big brass bed that they had. I came down on the bed rail, falling forward, and knocking my only permanent tooth out that I had at that time; you know the big one up front and it was dangling by a root. Dad pulled it out and put it in a paper towel. When he took Carol and I back home he handed mom my tooth. She was not happy with him. So by the time I was taken to a dentist, it was either too late to put it back in or maybe they didn't have the money, or maybe braces hadn't been invented yet. But anyway, I went without a front tooth and by the time I was old enough to get it fixed, I'd be about thirty years old. So I grew up without a front tooth. So thank God, this arrangement with all these kids in this apartment was only going to be temporary. Because you see, Ruby had six children, the oldest was on his way out and had gotten married; the next one in line was pregnant and would soon be married and gone so that left the rest of us. But soon Dad and Ruby would be married and Mom and Red would also be married. Dad moved his new family into a farmhouse in Lowville where my sister and I would get to see my dad on weekends. Mom and Red would live in the house that Dad built. So in July 1964, after living with Ruby for a year, Dad and she were married and Mom and Red were then married. So we would then go see our dad every weekend and stay with him and his new family in the rented farmhouse. The rented house had a lot to be desired. The indoor plumbing needed improvement for sure. I remember an outhouse out back that I was too scared to go in. But Dad wanted to live in the country and it was a start in the right direction. Since Dad loved horses as a kid he decided to start fencing off a corral for some ponies for us kids. Carol and I had to make a lot of adjustments at this time in our lives. Seeing those other kids on my dad's lap didn't make me happy. But Dad was doing his best to give these kids a decent home and he wanted them to love him as much as Carol and I did.

I remember Dad taking Carol and I with him to go look at a couple of ponies. My dad made it sound as if these ponies were going to be ours, so were happy thinking that perhaps that was what was going to happen. Well it didn't turn out that way, Dad just led us to believe that. He thought it would make us happy. So we went and looked at the ponies with the impression of them being ours, and guess what after he brought them home I never even got to be on one of them because the other kids were all over them all the time. The only ones on them were the three oldest ones. I guess he thought I was too young to know any better and it was obvious that two ponies wasn't going to be enough. Only we girls were interested in them. I think Dad tried to help us to get along and would try to get us together to play some games and stuff. Since we were all kids, we managed to get along okay. Dad would come out and play a game at night called "Kick the Can". He would always be the one who had to find us. I remember when I was the only one he couldn't find. Dad had this dump truck in the driveway and I was hiding under it. When I ran out and kicked the can and yelled, "Alli, alli in free" that meant we won and we all got to hide and Dad would have to look for us again. But what I didn't realize was that the truck leaked oil really bad and I was covered in oil. It was all over my back and everywhere.

Dad used to put us kids in the back of the dump truck and go drive around somewhere. It was fun being in the back of it. There was plenty of room for all of us and we could stand up and look out over the top of it with the wind in our hair. We felt like we were on top of the world. Except one day we were riding in the back of the it going down the highway when suddenly the dump bed starting going up with us kids standing up in the back of it. We were hanging on, screaming for dear life, when Dad finally pulled over and let the bed down since we were all dangling mid air. Apparently he accidentally hit a lever in the cab and didn't' realize what was happening, but it was fun while it lasted.

I don't think we had many pets back then. I do remember a basset hound. I didn't like that dog. It was lazy and you couldn't even play with it. So one day I was looking out the upstairs bedroom window and saw something in the tree out by the driveway. I didn't know what it was, so my sister I think said something to Dad about it. He went out and grabbed it. It was a raccoon! Dad put a leash and a collar on it and gave it to us kids to make a pet out of. I was very leery of it, and kind of kept my distance because it growled a lot and got mean. It didn't seem like anything I could cuddle. Some of the older kids could pet it, but it was a wild animal and the longer it was restricted the meaner it got. Dad eventually let it go. So Rocky, the coon, didn't last to long as our pet. Being a city kid, I could see this was not going to be a boring life. I would see Dad doing things I had never seen him do before.

There was always the matter of food to eat. What was he going to do to keep us all fed?

Well Dad got into butchering our own meat. There was a giant kettle in the backyard that I couldn't imagine what that was all about, until one day I saw this huge white hog hoisted up over the kettle. Dad was going to scald a Hog! There was water boiling in the pot (kettle) that Dad was lowering this huge animal (which dwarfed my dad in size) into; then he'ld scrape the hair and clean it off of it. This was something totally different than any of us had ever seen. I guess we were having pork for supper. I don't know if Dad took it somewhere else to be processed or if he did it himself. That part I don't remember, but at least we weren't going to starve. We would eat a lot of deer meat, too. Dad often poached deer to feed his family. So wild game was often on the menu. Ruby would cook up anything he brought home. Having to cook meals for all of us was job in itself for her. But Dad didn't just go out poaching the deer. There were many times he would go out with one of my uncles or one of us kids, and actually go hunting during the deer season. One story he would tell us was about a time when my Uncle Bud, Ross and he went out. There was big buck down in the gully where they often went hunting. The buck saw Dad and took off running. Dad go so excited that he didn't care if he had to sail one up that deer's ass, it was going down. So as the deer was running away, Dad took his shot, and "bam" that deer stopped, twirled around, fell down, got back up, fell down again and finally died. Dad shot that buck right in the balls. Boy, you know that had to hurt! I don't know of anyone else that would have taken that shot!

After Ruby and Dad got married, Dad told her he didn't want to have any more kids. He had all he could handle with joint custody of Carol and I and also having to support Ruby's remaining kids. But unfortunately Ruby told Dad two months after they were married that she was pregnant.

They lived together for a year and she never got pregnant. Anyway, Dad was not happy with this news and soon Ruby and he would start arguing. Dad didn't need any more mouths to feed. He was out poaching deer just to keep us fed. Then there was an issue with two of Dad's sisters who didn't want Dad to marry Ruby in the first place. So they chose not to speak to my Dad. So after this news was out about Ruby being pregnant, things started changing for all of us again.

So Dad went to the man that he was renting the house from and wanted to buy it. But the landlord wouldn't sell it so dad had to look for another house to live in. So a few houses down Dad found another farmhouse with five acres to move into. He had to figure out what the best way was to support his family. So the first thing he had to do was to make our house livable for all of us. The dining area would become a bedroom for Ruby, himself and "the golden child's" crib. The upstairs had two bedrooms and a bathroom with a tub and sink. So the three girls would stay in one side and my sister would stay in the other side with me. At least I had my own little bed to sleep in. Carol had her bed from our house and we both got to use one of our original dressers while my other dresser was given to Ruby's girls to use in the other bedroom. Richy didn't have a bed to sleep on so he slept on the living room couch. There was a closet partitioned off in the hallway so we girls would have somewhere to hang our clothes. I don't know where Richy kept his clothes. We know he had clothes but beats me where they were kept.

After all the sleeping arrangements were made, it was time to start the barn building. Dad laid boards out for the footer and soon our barn was in the making. The barn would have two sections. The first section was for the hay to be stored and the other section was for the animals. The older girls would get on the roof while we two younger ones would be "go fers". I was afraid of heights so I didn't get up on the roof. We even had to straighten out any bent nails to use in the barn. We all became carpenters at our young ages with me being the third from the youngest. Our age groups went from Roseanne, to Molly and Carol, Richy, me and then Shelly, and of course the golden child, Tim. We girls would help Dad build the barn out of used nails and lumber. So he and the oldest girls would go around tearing down old barns and garages and Dad started bringing used lumber to the farm and we girls would start pulling nails and stacking boards. A barbwire fence would be needed in the pasture. So we all learned how to put up fence, pound in fence posts and use electric saws to get the barn started. We used to pull slivers out of our hands all the time because we didn't have any gloves to wear. One time one of the girls was using the electric saw and sawed the cord in two. Dad came home and got mad but he spliced it back together and we continued on. It was the beginning of our hard and laborious lifestyle. We had to sort, stack measure and cut the boards. It was hard work. We still don't know how Dad set the beams for the barn, but he did. It had planking on the floors and he used 4 x 4 posts in it. It was going to be a damn fine barn. We know now that God was with my Dad giving him the strength and knowledge to give us the best life he could, which kept us out of trouble. I would always look back with no regrets. When it would come time to pour the footer for the barn, he would be out there with an electric cement mixer and a wheelbarrow pouring one section at a time till it was completed, step-by-step.

After awhile Dad would have enough horses or ponies for all of us girls eventually. Carol would eventually be given "Prince". "Little Lady" and he were the first horses we got and as we out grew them they would be passed down to the next kid. But Prince was kind of mean at first. A lot of times he would try to run Carol down when she went out to the pasture to get him. One time he bit her on her arm and left a big black and blue whelp on her. Of course we knew better than to cry to Dad about anything. Dad's rule was, "If you fall off, then get back on. Don't' cry, or I'll give you something to cry about." So when we got hurt, and if our arms and legs weren't broken then we better not say anything. But Dad eventually saw the bruise on Carol's arm. When he asked her what happened he grabbed a 2 x 4 for a club and went out to the pasture. When Prince came running at Dad, Dad Clubbed that horse across the head and Prince fell down on his knees. After that Prince turned out to be one of the gentlest horses we ever had.

We also had goats, ducks, chickens, geese, rabbits, pigs, dogs, a cat and a sheep. We raised beef and some of our other animals were harvested for food on the table. So in the morning we girls would go out in the barn and do the chores, feeding the horses and cattle, before we went to school. We loved our horses. They were a source of freedom for us since we lived out in the country where the neighbors were few and far between. We could saddle up and ride the back roads for hours. We also raised beef and once in awhile our bull would go through our electric fence to get at the neighbor's dairy cattle. When he went through the fence, the horses and other cattle would be running around the neighborhood with him. Sometimes Dad would whistle real loud and the horses would come running home, but we always had to go and get the bull. So Dad took matters into his own hands and decided to put rings in the bulls' noses. He told us kids to collect all the cobwebs out of the barn. This was supposed to stop the bleeding afterwards. Dad and a friend of his would catch the bulls and chain their heads to one of the horse stalls. Dad would grab that big ring and force it though that poor bull's nose. The cobwebs would get packed into their nostrils. Fortunately they didn't bleed enough to have to use the cobwebs. Besides those cobwebs were dirty. They would have whitewash all over them from us having to whitewash everything. Anyway, the nose rings worked pretty well. We could snap a chain on the end of the bull's nose and lead them around with one finger.

We also had two goats. Their names were Billy and Kid. Kid didn't have any horns, but Billy did. They would always rear up on their hind legs and butt heads. But when they played with us, they wouldn't come down on us or hurt us. One day I was out in the yard and I saw Dad walking towards the barn with a set of weird looking pliers, (called Bardizo's). I never knew what they were for until he went into the barn. The goats were in the barn and I heard the most horrible scream coming from one of the goats. Dad took those weird looking pliers and clamped it onto one of the goat's testicles and gave it a big squeeze. That goat's scream was so loud, "Baaaaaaaaa", and so long I knew that had to hurt. They walked a little stiff legged after that. But it didn't take with Billy. Before Dad could get to him to do it again, Billy got into a shed where Dad kept all of his bags of cement, ate cement and died. I remember going into the shed and seeing Billy dead on the floor. He was sprawled out and stiff as a board. I think you could have probably stood Billy up, he was so stiff. His eyes were a bright green. I guess eating the cement didn't agree with him. He would have rather died then get his nuts clamped again. Anyway after taking care of the bulls and confining them in the pasture on a chain, we didn't have to go through chasing them around anymore. So we thought. But one day we heard a bunch of horns honking on the highway we lived on. "Babe", (Molly's Holstein bull) was holding up traffic! There was a guy wearing a suit, standing outside his big white Lincoln, screaming at Molly to move that animal out of the street, or he was going to move him for her. So she just stepped aside and said, "Go ahead." So the guy came out from around his car door, took his jacket off and proceeded to move toward Babe! At that time Babe move toward the guy's front bumper and started sharpening his horns on the car. He was pawing at the ground with this tongue out making a bullish growling noise. The next thing we knew, that guy ran back into his fancy car and was pointing at the bull for us to get him off the road. So Molly took a rope with a snap on it and walked up to Babe and snapped the rope onto his nose ring and led him up the driveway and chained him back up in the pasture. Babe was Molly's pet. She could jump on his back and he never hurt any of us kids. She cried when Dad had to butcher poor Babe. She swore that she wouldn't eat any of the meat. But when that roast was set on the table she ate it just like the rest of us.

Ever since the baby was born, Ruby and Dad's arguing persisted to the degree where Dad would want to leave. He wasn't getting any attention anymore. It was all going to the baby and Ruby made it very clear to the rest of us that we were not to touch her son. When Dad went to go get Granma Brown, she would put the baby, (Tim), on such a pedestal. We didn't think she even knew the rest of existed anymore. So Tim grew up being known as the "Golden Child". Dad didn't believe in spoiling kids. We were all treated equally. Dad didn't give Carol and I any special treatment. Ruby was really strict with her girls too, while Richy could get by with anything. It was obvious that she favored the boys. There were times she would grab one of the girls by the hair, slap her and drag her around. Half the time she couldn't even hear what was going on and often would take things the wrong way because she was tone deaf in one ear and could barely hear out of the other. So we would practically beg Dad to get her a hearing aid. I remember one time I was going to be nice and feed her chickens and told her that I fed her chickens. She started coming after me, so I ran to Dad and told him what was going on apparently she thought I said F____ your chickens. So Dad made sure she had a hearing aid. I didn't want her beating up on me.

In the meantime the farm would take form and Carol and I would spend the summer and weekends with Dad. At the same time other things were going on at home. We found out that Mom had cancer. Even though she was getting radiations treatments, the cancer would slow down but wasn't going away. Since Red didn't have the money to continue the treatments, Mom was operated on at the time the cancer had spread elsewhere. The doctor gave her a hysterectomy, thinking it would remove the cancer, but instead made it worse. I remember Red having to bring home oranges and practice injecting them with a syringe because the cancer spread like wild fire as soon as they opened her up to try to remove the cancer. I remember her suffering and the vomiting every day in the bathroom. I guess the injections were morphine for the pain. The next thing I knew was after school I would always have to go the neighbor's house and wait there until someone came and got me. Mom wasn't home anymore. As a small kid at the age of eleven years old I knew Mom was sick. Back then the hospitals wouldn't let children in the rooms, so I didn't get to see my mom again until she was on her death bed, and even still they wouldn't let me in to see her. Someone had to sneak me in so she could say her goodbyes to us. I remember her leaning over the hospital bed and telling me to brush my teeth every day and to graduate from school. I told her I would and I did. Then one day I came home from school and Dad was sitting in the dining room and I knew something was different because Dad didn't live here anymore. That's when he took me by the hands and told me Mom was gone and went to heaven. She told my Dad before she went that she had met his God. We were at peace knowing that. I don't ever remember crying at her funeral. I think my aunt Marion took Carol and I to buy some dresses for the funeral. I remember it was summer time and my dress was a silky type of material with pastel colored pink, yellow, and blue flowers on it. As my sister and I made our way to take one last look at our mom in the casket we each bent over and gave her a kiss on her forehead. I'll never forget how cold and stiff she was when I kissed her. I knew then that the person in the casket was only a shell of my mom and she wasn't really in there. She died at the age of 36 on June 12, 1967. After the funeral my dad and Red worked it out so my sister and I could finish out the school year before my dad would take us into custody to live with him, Ruby and her children.

After our mom passed away my step dad turned into an alcoholic. Several times my sister and I would call the local bars to try and hunt him down. Sometimes we would be armed with butcher knives up our sleeves and have to comb through the local bars looking for him and begging him to come home. We knew Mom's death took a toll on him, but to drown his sorrows in beer when we needed him to be there for us wasn't going to solve anything. It was getting worse all the time. He would steal money out of my bank. My dad always gave us silver dollars and Kennedy half-dollars and every time I shook my bank it was lighter and lighter until he drank them all up. To top it all off he let his creep nephew stay with us and Carol and I spent half the time locking ourselves up in the bathroom trying to get away from him because we felt he would have tried to rape my sister if he could. We kept trying to tell Red about it, but it fell on drunken deaf ears, until one day he caught the bastard trying to break the bathroom door to get at my sister. I was in there too with her and the fight was on. My step dad grabbed him and while they were fighting in the hallway I thought I'd help (because I loved my step dad), and bit the hell out of who I thought was Frank, the nephew, and it turned out to be Red. Anyway Frank got tossed out the door and that's when I realized I bit the wrong man because my step dad was rubbing his hand and there was the perfect impression of my teeth on it. But soon the school year was up and Carol and I knew we had to go live with Ruby and Dad.

So after the school year was up, Carol and I moved in permanently with Dad and everyone at the farm, where life carried on as if nothing had happened. Carol and I were without the love and guidance that my mom provided. We got no hugs or kisses or any, "I love you's" from Dad. Ruby was too cold towards all of us except Richy and the Golden Child. So we relied on each other for moral support. All the animals we had seemed to fill the void we had. Plus Dad was too busy trying to get Ruby's kids to love him, so Carol and I could only sit back and watch. In the meantime Red never paid any of the taxes on my mom's house and it went up for foreclosure. Carol and I would get $1,000.00, a small box of trinkets that was my mom's, and a couple of pictures and that was it. I went into the sixth grade at a new school and Carol went into the ninth grade. Believe it or not, life went on. I relied on my sister to take the place of my mom. She was there when I needed her to be. I would often crawl in bed and sleep with her because I didn't have a mother figure around to ask any questions to. So we stuck it out and dealt with whatever life was going to hand us the best we could.

I never realized that we would never get to see our grandparents or aunts and uncles, or anyone on mom's side of the family again. Dad carried a grudge against Grandma Matthews, and thought that she was part of the reason why his and mom's marriage didn't work out. Of course we knew there was more to it than that. It wouldn't be until I was 21 before I would get to see any one on mom's side ever again. Unfortunately, my grampa would already be deceased by then. With him went all the knowledge of our Indian heritage. Later on in life I would have questions to ask that I knew only he could answer. So my dad was preventing us from seeing any of them.

Dad made us work and earn everything we had. We always had chores to do and a lot of responsibility was necessary in taking care of the animals. It was our duty to make sure things were taken care of; and we didn't get fed until all of our animals got fed first. In the summer time we kids used to give pony rides to help pay for our school clothes. We never really had any new outfits. They were mostly hand-me-downs. While the livestock tended to keep us pretty busy, my dad would always have something there at the farm to keep us kids occupied. We had an above ground pool we swam in, or we would go across the street into the neighbor's cow pasture and swam in the creek. I remember one time we were all swimming in the creek and it was pretty deep in some spots. But it was a nice swimming hole. I was swimming under the water and I was going to come up in the center of a tractor inner tube my sisters were hanging on to, and right when I came up for air in the center of it one of the girls shoved me back down into the water. I remember looking up and trying to swim back up to the surface but I couldn't and as I was going deeper, suddenly someone grabbed my arm and swiftly pulled me up. When I made it back to the surface I looked to see who had pulled me up and no one was there. After that I was afraid to go in to water over my head for a long time. I often wondered if my guardian angel was looking after me that day.

My dad also bought a couple of motorcycles for the older girls to have fun and ride around on. Most of the time they rode them around in the pasture, but one day they took them out on the back roads and got caught by a patrolman and were escorted home. I think their motorcycle days were over shortly after that. We also had some little foreign car we would drive around in the pasture. It was fun zooming around in that too. My dad also had a small speedboat. It was a wooden, red and blue boat with an outboard motor on it. He would pack us all up and take it on the lake, (Lake Erie). We would always race it into the waves the other bigger boats would make, and sail that little boat right out of the water. We would do that a lot when Dad was sitting in the back so he would get all wet. He was always doing that to us kids.

My dad was also a member of the Wattsburg Volunteer Fire Department. I don't remember if he was ever called out to put any fires out but the fire department would become a lifesaver for Dad in the years to come. You see the stress of having a big family would take its toll on my dad and he would suffer with heart attacks often. Apparently Dad had a ruptured valve and sometimes even just going down in the basement would bring on one of these attacks. I don't know how often Dad would be at the bottom of the basement stairs and we would have to grab his tongue to keep him from choking on it and put a Nitroglycerin pill under his tongue and wait for him to come out of the seizures. He had high blood pressure, too. It was hard for him to be the only sole supporter for our large family. Plus Ruby and he weren't getting along so great either, especially since Dad didn't want Tim spoiled. So there was always some kind of disagreement with that issue. When Dad would go and get his mom, (Granma Brown), Ruby and Granma would spoil Tim so bad that Granma didn't give the rest of her grandkids the same attention. Even my aunts would tell us how all Granma did was brag about the golden child to them, and how they would get upset about the extreme favoritism towards Tim and none towards the other grandkids. So the animosity would continue to be fueled by my step-mom and Granma Brown. My dad knew this and didn't have much say in the matter, so my dad paid more attention to the rest of us.

In the summer time when we weren't giving pony rides or riding the horses ourselves there was always something to do. Dad would always start water fights with us. He would start by sprinkling a little water on us and then it would blow out into a full-blown water battle with the girls getting the best shots in. It didn't matter if we were in the house or not, if Dad started it in the house it would get finished with Ruby yelling and all of us running outside. We had an old clock that the lens was broken out of and Dad would sit there with a straw and shoot spit wads at it until the big hand would get stuck.

We also had a Farmall tractor and when Dad would take it out we kids were either riding on it or we'ld use it to go pick up hay. A lot of times my dad would rent us out to the farmers, chopping corn stocks with machetes for our livestock to eat or we would bail hay for a percentage of the hay for our barn. We had more animals than we had pasture so we're having to feed our livestock all year round. There were times that the old tractor wouldn't start. Dad would have one of my sisters get in the truck, and they would have to pull the tractor and pop the clutch to get it started. One day, while Ruby and Dad were gone, we needed the tractor to fix the fence with or something. So Carol got in Dad's old 1950 Chevy truck and a friend got on the tractor. They were going to pull it down the highway to get it started. It was going okay until Carol had to swing the truck out to get up into our driveway. This idiot in a Corvette broadsided and knocked the truck into our fence in the front yard. My sister flew out of the truck, with the truck leaning on the fence over her. She was lying on the ground and I don't know what kept the truck from falling on her. But it didn't, thank God. But the guy in the Vet was a mess. I went over to help him, but he was mad and drunk and was calling us all kinds of names. We tried to tell him that the car was on fire, but he didn't want us anywhere near it. So we got some water from a pond nearby and threw it on the engine and left him there. Carol had to be taken to the hospital. She was banged and bruised up. I don't think anything was broken. I don't think Dad was too happy about it either. But there were a lot of things that Dad wasn't happy about.

He would often tell us to do things that we didn't know anything about. He just expected us to know and we didn't dare ask him how or why. So there were times we would work all day doing things that he wanted us to do and if it wasn't to his liking he would tear it completely down and remake it to his liking. He yelled at us so much that the donkey we had would start baying louder than Dad. Our donkey, "Apple Jack", would make an ass outta Dad every time he yelled at us outside of the house. It was no wonder he had heart problems. He never knew what it was like to come home from work and to just relax. Having a house full of kids made that impossible.

In the wintertime we would have to dig our way to the barn just to feed our animals every morning. There would be a path in the snow from the back door to the barn. Dad would have a water hose rigged up from the basement to the barn and we would always turn the water on to water our horses and cattle. Sometimes we would flood the barn by forgetting to turn it off. But we had a good system going on. We would let one horse out to drink at a time and after they were done they would know which stall was theirs and go right to it. Even when we opened up the barn to let them in they each knew right where to go. They would get fed twice a day, before and after school. The animals always ate before we did. But with every animal there would be sadness that we would have to deal with. We had three mares that had colts. Dad's horse had a filly that caught distemper and it stayed small and thin. Dad managed to save her but she never looked very healthy and later on was sold. We also had a small pony that had a little stallion colt. But the colt got tangled up in his stall because his chain was too long and I believe he had to be put down. Then one day I took my horse out for a ride and I didn't know she was pregnant. After I was done I noticed the milk dripping from her so dad told me to put her in the barn. That morning she seemed okay, so I went to school and didn't think anything of it. When I came home, my dad and cousin were in the kitchen. My dad proceeded to chew my butt out, telling me things like, "I hope you're happy. You should be ashamed of yourself. You go out there and see what you did to your horse!" So naturally I ran out to the barn with tears pouring from my eyes and went back to see my horse, and there was the prettiest colt ever. My horse had a little painted filly. I named her Shawny. But all was not well. My sister Carol had a large painted horse named Big Lady that was a show horse before we owned her. Big Lady had a dislocated hip. It didn't bother her though. She would still be a good horse to ride and my sister loved her. But one day my bull got loose in the barn and knocked Big Lady down and she couldn't get back up. Dad tried hoisting her up in the barn but she never did regain her footing so she had to be put down. My colt was given to my sister for what my bull had done. Then we had another horse named Little Lady. She belonged to my sister Molly. One day Little Lady got loose and went into the stall with my bull. When we came home from school, we all went out to do chores. Lady wasn't anywhere to be seen. When I went to feed my bull I found the horse all wadded up and smashed into the small space where his hay would have gone. After that Dad decided to get rid of the bull. He was too mean and couldn't be handled. So Dad traded him for a horse for me. Since we didn't have much pasture Dad would rent pasture from other people. One day my Dad's friend, who had a riding stable and boarded horses offered to rent some of his pasture to Dad. So we took our horses up there. When we let our horses in with the horses that were being boarded my horse named "Kit" got into a fight with one of the boarded horses and broke the other horses leg by kicking her. Unfortunately, my dad had to pay for the owner's horse. What I thought was odd was that the other horse looked identical to Kit. She was always bossing the other horses around. So there were a lot of things we had to deal with. With life comes death, and we kids learned to not get too attached to our animals. Even the little rabbits that were so cute when they were born, got knocked on the head and put on the dinner table. We just learned to accept it as a way of life.

My dad taught us all how to shoot. Since he had a gun collection. Dad put an addition on the house and opened up a gun shop, where he would sell guns and repair them. At the age of 12 I got my first rifle. It was a 22 caliber. All of us had 22s. Dad also did his own reloading. We kids would stay down in the basement for hours with Dad reloading bullets. We would always take the guns out and shoot them. Dad taught us all about gun safety. We would go out target practicing and hunting with him or go gravel road riding and shoot ground hogs out of people's pastures. He would whistle and the ground hog would sit up and we would blast it. Sometimes he would go out and hunt deer out of season, (poaching), just to keep us fed. He would always hit deer with the station wagons we had. There was always deer meat to eat. I remember one time when we were coming back from Erie and we saw a hunter on the side of the road standing over a huge eight point buck. So Dad pulled over to check it out. He had a couple of us kids with him that day. As he approached the hunter Dad congratulated him on such a nice deer. We couldn't help but notice the hunter was a green horn with his new hunting outfit on and his new gun.

When the guy told us the deer wasn't his, he had just come up on it, my dad took out his pocketknife and cut into the hide and smelled it and then tasted it. He told the hunter it was gangrene. The guy jumped back away from the deer and left, like he was scared of it. So as soon as he left my dad, sisters and I loaded that big buck up in the back of the station wagon and took it home. There wasn't anything wrong with it. My dad conned that guy to get that deer and it worked. After that, my dad proudly displayed the rack on the wall and we all called it the gangrene deer antlers.

We had fun in the wintertime too. Dad would build his snow forts and take us kids tobogganing. He would take us to the gravel pit, which was very steep and scary. I went down it once and got hurt enough for me not to want to go down it again. Then Dad went backwards down it on the sled before he was ready and nearly broke his neck. He had to have his neck in a brace for a long time after that. He must have thought we were all invincible. Safety was definitely not an issue back then. Instead of us risking our lives on the slipper slopes, Dad built this huge sled, big enough for all of us and painted it yellow. We named it the "Blue streak" after a roller coaster at the amusement park he would take us to in Ohio. He would pull it behind the tractor out on the back roads in the wintertime and it was a blast. We got as much use out of that tractor as we could. Dad would take us on hayrides around the neighborhood. When friends came over there was always some form of entertainment. We would shoot the guns, ride the horses, go for hayrides, or just go around and pet the animals. Our farm had more of variety than a petting zoo. You would be surprised how many people would try to feed our goat tin cans. It was crazy. But it taught us discipline and responsibility.

Even when it rained out Dad managed to entertain us somehow. When it rained in Pennsylvania it poured. So Dad would take the opportunity to take a shower out in the rain. He would be out there in nothing but his undershorts, soaping himself up. We would watch him from the windows and after he would get all soaped up, it would quit raining and he'd be out there cussing, like the sailor he was. We would be in the house laughing. But eventually it would start raining again and he would get rinsed off. You see there was no shower in any of the houses we had; just a bathtub upstairs. Although Dad always bragged about the Artesian well we had, he would never let us wash our hair or take a bath more than once or twice a week. So most of the time we would just go upstairs and wash up, so we didn't go to school smelling like the barn. But when my brother Richy had to take a bath upstairs, it was utter chaos. None of us girls could go up to our bedrooms, and we would sit downstairs for hours waiting for him to come down. You See Dad didn't believe in privacy. Neither the bedrooms nor the upstairs bathroom had anything over the doorways. No curtains or even a sheet or blanket. Anyone could come up at anytime. Ruby would do that often because that's where the girls' rooms were. Richy would always fall asleep in the bathtub and we would always have to get Ruby to go up there and wake him up. So it was a problem for us girls to not have any doors on the two bedrooms we shared and the upstairs bathroom. It was very intimidating for us since there was no such thing as privacy.

Sometimes when it rained our pasture would flood. It wasn't enough to hurt anything but it was enough to have fun in. One time Dad went out with us and we would play out in the water and ride the horses through it. We seemed to find some sort of fun in just about anything we could. Sometimes the rains would knock the electric fence out and we would have to walk around with the fence tester and look for the break or short in the fence. Sometimes it would be something as simple as a weed being to tall and shorting it out, or there would be a definite break in the wire. One time the fence went out and Dad had to go out and fix it. It had just rained and puddles were everywhere. The fence was broken right by the barn and Dad was out there with a hammer and some tools, while one of the girls was in the doorway of the barn and I was at the switch, which turned the fence off and on. Dad was talking to my sister, Roseanne, who was standing in the door waiting to give me instruction on when to turn the fence on. I guess you know where this is going. Well, I asked Roseanne if Dad said "turn the fence on" and she said "yes", so I turned the fence on. Boy did I hear him yelling out there, cussing like a mad man. I came out of the barn and there was Dad standing in a water puddle with one hand on one end of the fence and the other hand was holding the other end of the fence. He couldn't let go of the fence, so I ran back in and shut the fence off as fast as I could. But that wasn't good enough for Dad. He was armed with a hammer as he came after me and the only thing that saved me was the fact that I could jump over the fences and he couldn't. I must have run a half a mile down the road before he gave up and cooled down enough to keep him from whooping my ass.

At about this time Dad pulled Carol and I aside and would have a request for us. He wanted us to start calling Ruby "Mom". I know in my heart and in Carol's heart that this was something we didn't want to do. No one was going to take the place of our mom, and he knew it. But I guess he wanted us to do it for her. So we did, with the feeling of reluctance, since

Ruby showed no love for even her own kids except for the golden child. But Dad wanted to have his family to be complete. However, we never heard any of our siblings calling him Dad. Richy came out and said Dad was the closest thing he ever had to a real father. So although it got easier to call her Mom, it still left us uncomfortable. But we loved our dad and would respect his request.

When holidays and birthdays rolled around we all knew better than to ask for anything because we knew that Dad didn't have money to spend on everyone. With so many of us living under the same roof, we didn't know how to keep track of everyone's birthday, anyway. So Dad would buy some ice cream and one of the girls would bake a cake and every weekend we had ice cream and cake. If it was someone's birthday then we would put some candles on the cake. After the candles were blown out we would set them aside for the next birthday. As far as holidays went the big meal on the table was as much as we got and we didn't complain about it either. Except one year, I think is when Dad gave us all our 22's for Christmas. So we never expected anything. About the only thing we did expect for Christmas was a Christmas tree. One year Dad was slacking on getting us a tree to decorate and no matter how much we asked, it would fall on deaf ears. So at the farmhouse Dad had four very nice Blue Spruce Trees that lined the left side of the driveway that he seemed pretty proud of. While he was napping on the living room couch one day, instead of stealing the neighbor's trees, my sisters went outside with a hack saw and cut off one of Dad's trees that was on the end. We dragged that tree into the living room and set it up and decorated it right there. He never woke up. When he did wake up he asked us where we got the tree. I don't think he got a straight answer, but he thought it was a really nice looking tree all decorated and everything. So I guess he was led to believe that we just found it and cut it down or stole it from someone else's property, until one day he came home from work and noticed one of his beautiful Blue Spruces was missing. He was going to chew our butts out but Ruby told him it was his fault for not getting us a Christmas tree. So after that Dad made sure we had a tree for Christmas. Even if it was an artificial one, it didn't matter. If nothing else, we were going to have a Christmas tree for Christmas and that was that.

Since Dad did reloading he would teach us how to operate the reloading press. Dad always loaded the ammunition a little on the "hot" side. Many times he would fire a round or two in the basement to see how it shot. I remember the piles of dirt in the basement. Even though I call it a basement, it was more like a root cellar. You had to bend over to get the door open and that's probably why Dad having high blood pressure, we would often find him at the bottom of the stairs. Anyway there were times a reload would be too hot and I remember one of the cylinders off of the 38 special having a big crack in it. I think Carol was the victim of shooting that one that time. So Dad put a dummy bullet in that spot until he got another cylinder for it. He shot guns like they were toys. He would shoot them in the cellar and shoot them in the kitchen floor. If we left the light on in the basement you could see a beam of light coming up through the kitchen floor. Thank God none of us were down there at the time. It's a wonder we weren't all deaf either. This all seemed like normal activities to us, so we never thought anything of it at the time.

One day out of the blue my step-dad showed up and Dad met him outside. Red was drunk and wanted Carol and I back. Well, that wasn't going to happen and Dad and he got into it. My step-dad had his own kids that he never paid any attention to. So Dad thought he would scare Red away by going in the house and getting a rifle. It was just a 22 caliber, (Richy's gun). When Red wouldn't leave, Dad cracked him over the skull with the stock of the gun. I didn't want Red hurt, I just wanted him to leave so Dad wouldn't hurt him. Red wound up with blood running down his face. When he left we didn't see him anymore, until about forty years later.

Sometimes in the summer Dad would let a few of us kids go into work with him. He would drop us off at Bush and Phillis' house because the mall was only a couple of blocks from where they lived. We kids would spend the day at the mall looking around, and then Dad would pick us up when he got off work. Well, I can remember one day sitting at their kitchen table and hearing something scurrying around in their cabinets above my head. I naturally thought it might have been a mouse. Boy was I surprised when I cracked the kitchen cabinet door open to find out that it wasn't a mouse at all. Instead it was one of the biggest cockroaches I had ever seen, dragging a sugar cube across the shelf. I had always thought about popping one of those sugar cubes in my mouth. Thank God I never did. And there were a couple of times on the way home Dad would stop and buy some goodies. We would share on the car ride home. One time he had some "Ready Whip", and we would have fun squirting in each other's mouths before we got home. I also remember a "Rotisserie Chicken" we scarfed down before we got home so Ruby wouldn't find out. Dad was a big man, tipping the scales at over 300 pounds. So I could imagine how hungry he would have gotten after working in a hot shop all day, and he didn't mind sharing with us. But we had to keep quiet about it. Ruby wasn't very understanding at that time and would always frown at us and criticize us for wanting to have fun. Her favorite line was, "Why don't you grow up?' Since she was no fun, Dad would lean more towards us kids, because that's what he was, a big kid.

After Roseanne got her driver's license, Dad would let her take us to the mall. One time we all got in the station wagon to leave and Roseanne couldn't get the car to go forward. It would go in reverse, but not forward. I don't know how long we sat in the mall parking lot, wondering if the ol' wagon was broken down. But Dad came to the rescue; got in the wagon and took the emergency brake off. Then we were able to go home. It didn't take him long to figure it out.

There were times when he would gross us out too. Dad had a gap between his two front teeth. If we weren't paying any attention to him, he would yell out to one of us and gross us out with his amazing talents. One time he took spit and forced it through his front teeth, and it would whip all over his face and then he'd suck it back in. Of course we were grossed out. So one day my sister Carol did the same thing to him" and he gagged and ran to the bathroom. We thought he was going to barf before he made it. So he didn't do that to us any more. Then when he ate spaghetti he would do the same thing with the spaghetti noodles. His face would be all spattered with spaghetti sauce. Or he would see how fast he could suck his spaghetti through his two teeth and the sauce would be down his chin and on his shirt. He liked showing off, so he didn't mind making a mess, even if it was at the table. It didn't bother him to embarrass us at any public places either. But we always got him back.

Our neighbor had a dairy farm across the street from us. We kids were always going over there to play in the creek or we would go catch crawdads or go fishing. (Before we got the swimming pool,) we would go swimming. It was all cow pasture and the guy who owned it didn't mind us being over there. Usually if we went fishing, we would always out fish Dad. He would cheat and run us out of our fishing holes. One day the only thing Dad caught was a tiny perch. So I stuck it down through the neck of the milk jug and brought it home and put it in a small fish bowl that I had. It was a bit of an embarrassment for Dad, but it was a cool fish. After I put it in clean water its color would come out. I had it trained to jump out of the water for a dead fly. Since we had enough flies in the house, Dad always hung those nasty flypaper strips from the ceilings. I used to hate getting those things caught in my hair. Since I was tall someone would always pull the damn thing all the way out. Anyway my fish was pretty interesting until someone put paper in its fish bowl and suffocated it. But we always had fun exploring around that whole area. There was always skunk cabbage that grew wild all over the place over there and once in awhile we would go over and kick it to make it stink. One time there was this old cow carcass I walked up on and a possum ran out of it, that was kinda cool. I remember Dad had a friend over one day and they talked Molly and Carol into going over there to go snipe hunting. Sometimes Dad would fool us kids and send us on a wild goose chase. It was their turn. So Carol and Molly went across the street with their burlap sacks and a couple of sticks. The sticks were used to beat the trees with and they would call to the snipes. I guess the snipe was supposed to fly into the bag. I don't know how long the girls were gone, but dad and his friend must have gotten a good laugh. The girls came back empty handed. The girls didn't care, it gave them a chance to get away for awhile.

Since all the kids were out fishing Dad, he decided he and I would go out one time just the two of us. Surely he could out fish a little kid like me. So Dad took us to a bridge overlooking a big creek. I could see the fish in the water swimming around. Dad put some bait on my hook and before he could bait his hook, I had a big fish hitting on mine. We had these big fish up there that we called white suckers. I think they were related to the carp family. I just lowered my line down there amongst them and bobbed it around and one of the big fish took it. The fish was so big that Dad had to walk the fishing pole off the bridge and go down to the bank to reel it in. He put it in a five-gallon bucket and its tail hung out over the top. After that Dad wouldn't take me fishing again. I don't remember eating any of my fish. We did used to have fish in our swimming pool though. Back then we didn't use any chemicals so some of the fish we brought home would go into the pool, unless they were sucked up in the fire hose trucks. That's where we got our pool water from. Anyway, it was cool having the fish in the pool. If ya stood still, the fish would pick at any moles or freckles ya had. It was fun swimming with the fish. They ate the bugs outta the pool. We got to swim in fish poop, but we didn't care.

It wasn't hard for us kids to keep ourselves occupied. We were a close-knit family at that time. Since the animals were in the barn most of the winter, that meant the barn needed cleaned out regularly. Every day we girls would have to shovel out the stalls and put down fresh straw so the livestock's' hooves wouldn't rot. The box stalls would get cleaned out a few times during the winter. Sometimes we would have to shovel the snow out from in front of the big doors just so we could get the animals out in the pasture so we could clean out all the stalls. We would have to shag the horses out in the snow and they would stand outside the door waiting to come back in. I didn't mind cleaning the barn out. Sometimes one of us would get hit with a pitchfork of manure and the next thing ya know we would have manure everywhere. But we always cleaned it up. Dad put a window at the other end of the barn to pitch the manure out of and when the pile got big enough, he would hook the manure spreader up to the tractor and spread the manure around the pasture to fertilize it. The manure spreader was a rickety old thing that had a handle to operate it. Dad would rig a rope onto it so he could pull it while he was on the tractor. But sometimes it wouldn't work, so he would mess with it trying to get it to work with one of my sisters on the tractor. When it started working, Dad would get manure flying at him.

My dad always had station wagons. Some of them were the big nine passenger wagons. I remember he had this 1960 Ford wagon that he was always patching up. (Because the winters were so harsh, the county would put salt on the roads.) So my sisters offered to paint it. Dad gave my sisters paintbrushes and paint and let them have at it. While Dad was napping my sisters proceeded with the paint job. Now this was the year of Woodstock and hippies, to trust my sisters with painting the family car; well let's just say I don't think I would have trusted them. Anyway, I don't even know where the colors came from they used. I thought we only had whitewash around the house. But they got it painted and I don't think I've ever seen so many daisies on one vehicle before. Dad didn't have any choice but to drive it to work. Boy did he get harassed by his buddies at work. He was so embarrassed. Of course, we didn't think anything about it. We thought it was cool! The nicest wagon my dad ever had was a 1965 Pontiac Catalina nine passenger. It had as much chrome on the inside as it did on the outside. One day it needed towed home. Dad had it hooked up to the truck, towing it home and one of my sisters was driving it, trying to keep it on the road. But the chain broke and the wagon along with my sister went over an embankment. That took care of that car. Dad ended up selling it to a young guy so he could have the motor for his racecar.

As we girls were getting older, there was of course going to be boys around. Since the oldest girl, Rosella, got pregnant and had to get married at the age of 15, Dad was going to make sure the rest of us girls wouldn't be in that same situation. He was very protective with the rest of us. Boys were not an issue for me. They weren't interested in a skinny, under developed girl like me. But the rest of my sisters, even Shelly, was far more advanced with their bodies than I was. My dad had a way of putting us in categories. There were the three oldest: Roseanne, Carol, and Molly; and the three youngest, Richy, Shelly and me. So when one of the oldest got in trouble or one of us younger ones got in trouble; he would punish all three of us. So when Richy or Shelly would do something they weren't supposed to, then I would get punished along with them. I didn't have any interest in boys, but Shelly and Roseanne were both boy crazy, so you can see what I'm getting at here. Richy was always getting grounded for not doing what he was told and Ruby would let him do what he wanted anyway, (because he was a boy), so there was some issues with that. Shelly would stay at her girlfriends' houses overnight to be around the boys. So when our phone would ring and Dad would find out what was going on, he would take action. The first thing he would do was to build a cage around the phone and put a lock on it so no one could use it to call their boyfriends with. But of course that didn't work. So one of my sisters was going down to our garage, (which was built into the hillside in front of the house), by going out the upstairs window in the middle of the night to meet her boyfriend. I guess our dog gave them away. Dad was suspicious and grabbed the 357 magnum and went down to the garage and caught one of my sister's boyfriends down in the garage. He pointed the gun at the kid's head and told him that he could shoot him for trying to steal the car. So the boy confessed and that pretty much took care of the boy situation.

Dad had a heck of a time trying to keep all of us kids in line. While Ruby decided to slap the crap out of her girls when they sassed back' Dad took a different approach to getting information from us and deciding what kind of discipline we got. He would make us put our hand on the Bible, and then start interrogating us like we were in a court of law. If he thought we were lying then he would threaten to take our horses away from us. Since our horses were our only source of freedom, we weren't going to do anything to jeopardize that. However, since my brother Richy didn't care about the horses, he didn't mind lying on the Bible, so Dad knew better than to question him.

Dad didn't mind coming to school and checking on us either. He had a rule about us girls having to wear our skirts or dresses to the middle of our knees. It was the middle of the Vietnam War, Rock and Roll and min-skirts; so after we got to school, those skirts were getting rolled up. So Dad would come to school while classes were changing and if any of us got caught, then we would get paddled. If we got paddled at school, then we would get paddled at home. Since I got paddled at school by Dad with a paddle with holes drilled through it, I gave up wearing skirts. Since I was the tallest, I couldn't wear my sister's skirts anyway, but they could wear mine. So all the clothes that were in our closet, (which was in the middle of the house downstairs), I let my sisters have. I didn't want my dad to have any more grief than he already had. Besides I didn't want my ass paddled again. Even though it hurt like hell, I made sure I wasn't going to cry, no matter what. So I made sure I wouldn't get caught by dad again and it saved me a lot of grief in the long run, too.

Now back to the garage, I guess it was an earth contact garage. We could walk on it from the back side. We used to make snowmen in the winter time and put them on top of the garage so when people would drive by they could look up and see them from the highway. We lived right off the main road in a small town called Lowville. I can remember Dad coming home and parking in the garage. We kids would make a bunch of snowballs and wait for him to come home. I remember we made this big snowball one time and when Dad came out from the garage, we kids would be on the roof ready to blast him. First we rolled the big snowball on him. That got him staggering around, then we would throw the other ones at him and run like hell, leaving him out there in the snow. We would dig tunnels in the snow too. We would get so much snow that our cars would be buried and all you could see would be the antennas sticking up out of the snow. We had snow blowers instead of plows to clear the main highways but if you lived on a gravel road then you were out of luck, which is why we had a lot of snow days. We had an Arctic Cat dealer who lived behind us, so a lot of people got around with snowmobiles. We didn't have a snowmobile but dad's friend did and he would come out and give us rides on it. I liked the snowmobiles. I remember one time we were waiting for Dad to come to the dinner table. We waited for him for a while and couldn't figure out what happened to him, so we stuck our heads out the door. We could hear him but couldn't see him. Well, he had fallen in one of our tunnels in the snow, and couldn't get out. So we had to put the ladder in there so he could climb out. He said he got snow blind and didn't see it. But that was after he cooled down and quit cussing, of course.

In the meantime during all that was going on in our lives Dad still suffered with the heart attacks. The Wattsburg Fire Department's rescue truck would always be there with oxygen to help us revive him. It was getting to be a constant problem for Dad and us. We would never know if it was going to be the last time we'd see him or not. But we all knew that

God worked in mysterious ways and he had a plan for my dad. Although we didn't go to church that much, my dad would always preach to us to fear God and him, and believe me, we did.

Now I guess I should talk some about our school we went to, Wattsburg School. It had the worst school spirit ever. The kids never cheered at any of the pep rallies, probably because they would never win a game. Dad would let us go to the football and basketball games but for me it sucked. I don't care for ball games to this day. The three oldest got to stay for the dances afterward, but the three younger ones, which included me had to be ready to leave at 10 o'clock to meet Dad out in the parking lot. That really sucked because I didn't care about the stupid games. I wanted to dance. I loved to dance and sometimes we girls would have a transistor radio or play records and do line dancing to rock and roll in the kitchen. I always thought I was a pretty good dancer for a skinny kid. But dad didn't like our rock and roll music and always played country music in all the speakers he had rigged up all around the house. Sometimes our transistor radios would go on the blink, and since Dad was such a handyman, we would make the mistake of taking our radios to him to fix. Well, he would fix them all right, to where they wouldn't work anymore. I used to listen to mine at night because I could get more stations in, like WLS out of Chicago. There was a radio show called, "WLS Boogie Check". It was cool. There would be people calling requesting songs. It was cool for back in those days. But at night Dad would flip a switch and we would have to sleep with that damn country music on.

As time went on we were all growing up and becoming young adults. My sister, Roseanne, would soon be graduating. She and my dad's friend, Chaz, (who was not much older than Roseanne), were seeing each other regularly. I think Chaz knew that the way to get to Roseanne was to be Dad's sidekick. He always helped Dad patch up our vehicles, and once in awhile he would give us a ride in his cool cars. He had a Red Fairlane with a four-speed in it and then he had a 1970 Torino. It was grabber-green. Everyone liked Chaz. He was a loveable guy. Roseanne and he wanted to get married but Dad kept postponing things, making them wait all the time. So they kept hanging in there and tried to be patient. But the wait was over and she and Chaz eloped and it created a problem with Dad. He wanted to control that situation, and when he couldn't, he chose to not talk to them for a long time. Eventually, Roseanne would have their first child and Ruby stood up and told Dad she wanted to see her grandbaby. Dad gave in and things were okay after that. Roseanne and Chaz had a mobile home out on his parent's place and Dad and Chaz senior became real good friends. We would often go to their farmhouse, which wasn't too far from where we lived. After that it was Carol and Molly's turn to graduate. They both had boyfriends too. Carol was engaged to a boy a year younger than her so they would have to wait until after he graduated before they could get hitched. Molly had a steady beau, who was also a year younger than her, but they were friends and didn't have any plans for marriage. It seemed every guy Molly was with would be intimidated by how well she could out shoot, out ride, out wrestle and just plain out do them.

Sooner or later our lives would have to change again. As we grew up Dad and Chaz were still poaching deer together. They were like a pair of outlaws out at night, I guess one night they may have gone too far. Dad knew he could never go to jail because of the mouths he had to feed. As if it wasn't bad enough including Granma Brown at the dinner table, Dad would pick up other people and bring them home, too, like the three Mexicans that he invited over. Dad had a big heart and sometimes he didn't realize that he wasn't a very good judge of character. He always prayed for and brought home people who were less fortunate than we were. Although that's not a bad thing, it would sometimes backfire on him. The little Mexican guys were a lot of fun. They would go swimming with us and it seemed pretty innocent at first until they started looking at the older girls in a different way. I don't know if they were just passing through or Dad ran them off.

Then there was a girl whose parents were very poor and Dad would often go and help them out. She had epilepsy, and there were times we would be playing cards and suddenly she would plop on the floor and have an epileptic seizure. We would just freak out and couldn't do anything until she came out of it. I think it was just getting too risky having her there. Although we felt bad for her, she couldn't do anything for fear of having another seizure all the time. So she was always confined to the house and we had to be confined with her. It was a real drag. Then there was a family whose daughter I went to school with. I don't know how Dad knew them. But they were my girlfriend's aunt, uncle, and grandmother who lived next door to her. Her aunt and uncle were brother and sister. He always gave me the creeps. Well Dad would go over to their house and help replace the roof on their house and would invite Lony, (the uncle), over to the house all the time. He would always gawk at me and I always felt like he was trying to undress us girls with his eyes. Then rumor had it that he was sleeping with his sister. I knew my girlfriend always joked around about how they were a buncha inbreeds, but I never took it seriously. Lony's sister was a very shy woman and never talked much, so I thought they were kinda weird.

Well to get back to the poaching. Chaz and Dad were like outlaws as I started saying earlier. One day the constable came to our house. Although they had no proof of what Dad and Chaz were doing, they warned Dad that he would be watched and if caught it would be a prison sentence. Apparently they did get caught, but because it was dark, Dad couldn't be identified in the assault of possible two game wardens, who were beaten up pretty badly, enough for one to be hospitalized. So in the summer of 1972 Dad took a long vacation to go around the other states looking for another place to live. I can't recall who went with him but he ended up in Jefferson City, Missouri. Soon he would be selling all the horses but two of them. All the other animals had to go to other homes as well, except the dogs. It would be a long haul to Missouri with three trucks and trailers making up the caravan. Dad got in touch with a realtor that would give us temporary housing until the rock farmhouse was ready to move into. So although we were moving to Missouri, not everyone would be living there. Rich ended up joining the Marines. Carol was working and waiting to be married, Molly was going out on her own, and Shelly thought living with her alcoholic Dad would be better, since she never loved my dad, anyway. So that left Ruby, Dad, the golden child and me.

After reaching our destination, we had to stay in a house on Bald Hill Road. It would be about three months before our house would be ready to move into. So the first thing Dad would have to do is get a job. He was hired right away at Westinghouse. But this job would be temporary until the state maintenance job was available. Without all the other kids around, Dad would grow up as we did. After the house was ready to move into he would then register Tim and I at the public schools. The rock house looked big on the outside but was very small on inside. The walls on the outside were very thick because of the stonework on the outside. Since the house was 100 years old they didn't need a lot of space to live a century ago. The kitchen had shelves for the dishes to go on and wasn't big enough for a kitchen table. There was no heat or air upstairs and it would get too cold or too hot for sleeping. So Dad built an addition on the back porch area eventually. I'm glad he did because I fell off it one night and it was one hell of a drop. It also had a cistern, (underground well), and the water we bathed and drank was either bought or came from the rain gutters that were directed into it. Although it had a furnace, there were only a few registers. Since Ruby was always sitting on them hogging the heat,

Dad decided to put a wood stove in. We also had five acres for the horses. The pasture needed some work. Dad and I would be out in it all the time picking up rocks. I had never seen a place so full of rocks before. The weeds took over the place. Even the yard was neglected. We could hardly see the out building. There was grass to knock down, with the horses help, and rocks all over the yard. Since Tim was too busy whining to Ruby, the job was up to Dad and I. After picking up rocks all day, Dad and I discovered that Missouri had chiggers. This was something I had never heard of and we would be covered with bites. The ticks about sucked all the blood out of us, but we kept on trucking. There were also snakes here that I wasn't familiar with. One day I went out to the garage and I heard something hissing at me from behind. I turned around and there was a snake with its head all spread out in a striking pose and I screamed and ran in the house. I told dad, "They have cobras here, there's one in the garage!" Dad told me I was full of shit and came out to investigate it. It turned out to be a Hognose Snake, and Dad picked it up with the pitchfork and threw it over the fence. Hognose Snakes look similar to rattle snakes but are harmless, and will often play dead if threatened. The back of the garage had a separate storage area and one day I was going out to get something for Dad and a snake fell off the roof onto me and scared me. It turned out to be a poisonous snake and its mate was still on the roof, so Dad killed it and went looking for the other one, but never found it. I don't remember if it was a Copperhead or a small rattler at the time.

Riding the school bus was a challenge in itself. Tim started fighting on the bus about every day. He would bully the other kids and I was always having to do something with him to try to make him behave. But he was too spoiled from Ruby babying him. He would come home and tell lies and try to get me in trouble all the time. One day we got kicked off the school bus because he was the kid from hell. At least that was what the pink slip read. So Dad was out there that very next day to put us right back on the bus. I remember Dad having to come to school one day because the school didn't approve of my clothes. I'm tall and sometimes my shirts wouldn't cover my belly completely when I wore my hip huggers. Apparently they didn't approve and sent me home with a note. So Dad went to school and told the principal that if they didn't like my clothes than they could buy them for me from now on. So right away they targeted me at school. There was a time I was in the girl's restroom and some girls were in there smoking and I accidentally knocked someone's cigarette off a shelf. When I bent over to pick it up a teacher came in and caught me picking it back up. She wanted me to walk down the hall carrying it and I refused, so I got a three-day suspension. Well Dad was right back in the school telling them that I didn't smoke and what had happened. Once again I was back in school. So I didn't get started off on the right foot.

Soon it would be winter and Dad ordered some wood to split. We would be out there with a wood splitter splitting wood and stacking it on the front porch. The winters here were very mild compared to what we were used to. There were times we would go out to meet the school bus, and there wouldn't be any school. Or the bus driver would stop and pick us up, take us to school and he would have to bring us back home. So they would close down schools for practically nothing. But we got more ice than snow, so I guess the back roads were bad.

Dad being a deer hunter had to find a place to hunt. So he would just trespass on other people's property not thinking they would care, but found out they did care around here. Deer season was a big deal in this state and Dad often found himself trespassing on farmers' property. So he set out to meet his neighbors to get their permission. So while the season was still open Dad and I set out to hunt on the neighbor's property up the road, who's property cut way back in behind ours. Dad and I found a path in the snow of fresh deer tracks and proceeded to follow them. There must have been a herd of deer running up over the next ridge, so naturally we were excited and couldn't wait to sneak up on them. The whole time we were walking slowly trying to be quiet and stay out of sight so he could get a good shot at one. All that time were thinking about how there must be a lot of deer in Missouri. As we got closer to the top of the ridge there was fresh deer poop everywhere, so we hunkered down as we got to the top to look over and see if this herd of deer were there. Wouldn't you know it; we were following a bunch of goats the whole time. As I gave Dad that look of "you dummy", he said, "Well damn it, how was I to know there were goats out here." As we walked all the way back to the house, I asked, "I thought you were the great white hunter?" He said, "Smart ass, don't tell Ruby." Then continued calling himself a dumb ass, not believing we had walked that far all morning long, just to have our adventure ruined by a bunch of damn goats. But that was okay, I was with Dad and that's all that mattered. It snowed on us all the way back home, so we told Ruby we quit because of the snow.

Since we moved to a rural area, everyone around us had several acres of land. Dad was always willing to help out his neighbors for some hunting privileges. But since Dad was never a very good judge of character and always felt bad for people less fortunate than us, sometimes his choices of friends weren't all that great. Across the street down a steep hill was a family of people who lived in a little shack with dirt floors. Although they had several acres it seemed odd to me that their home was not much better than our chicken coop. Dad took pity on them and would offer his support; if there was anything he could do for them to not hesitate for them to call. The family consisted of an 80 year old couple and their alcoholic son: who was in his 40's and the son's granddaughter. Well, the next thing we knew the son was calling us all the time for Dad to take him to town for groceries, which consisted of alcohol, and then he would invite himself over to the house all the time, which made me very uncomfortable. So I would disappear every time. Then it happened, he called Dad up and told him that he would like to take me out sometime! Well, needless to say, we didn't see him any more.

Then there was another guy Dad helped out that was a deaf mute. The only word he could say was the "F" word. After Dad invited him to the house one day, the deaf mute ended up stealing Dad's truck battery and $20 off the bedroom dresser. I told him that I wished he wouldn't bring these people home.

Then he decided to buy a CB radio and joined a CB club. He got familiar with this one guy who called himself "The Rim Rock Cowboy". While Mr. R. C. perceived to give the impression that he was some kind of over-the-road trucker, all the truck drivers were getting mad at him for telling them that there weren't any "smokies" up ahead and that they could put the pedal to the metal, when in fact the "smokies" were out there pulling everyone over. Dad decided to get to know this Rim Rock person, not knowing anything about him. So they talked frequently over the main base CB that Dad had and the one in his pickup truck. Rim Rock talked Dad into coming out and picking him up one day. I had no idea what was going on, I was in the back seat when Dad pulled up to where this guy lives, and out came some crippled up dude from a broken down trailer, that had to sit next to me in the back seat of the station wagon. I, once again, gave dad "that look" in his rear view mirror. After carting Mr. Rim Rock all over town, we went back home and Dad realized that Mr. RC cowboy was nothing but a liar and how he had gotten thrown out of the CB club for the false info that he was passing on to the truckers. So once again although Dad thought he was being thoughtful and considerate, it always seemed to backfire on him.

After we had lived here for several months, Roseanne and Chaz moved down here and rented a house just up from us. Richy would be coming home from the Marines on an honorable discharge. His asthma would be the reason for that. The Marines called it, "controlled breathing", so when he came home we would go out and run around a little together. Then he met Ellen and got married, and they had a son and settled down in Jefferson City. Dad didn't care too much for Ellen because she wasn't used to seeing so many guns in the house and didn't want Richy to go hunting. I don't think he was big on the sport anyway. So Dad and Chaz would pal up and go out hunting every now and then.

In the summer time Dad volunteered me to baby-sit the neighbor's little boy. I didn't want to do it, but I did for a few extra bucks. I was the lousiest baby sitter ever, but they didn't seem to care, just so someone was there with their kid every day. So that would preoccupy my time during the day. But after school started back up, I got hired at Wal-Mart part-time. Sometimes I would have to walk to Wal-Mart from school. But fortunately, I could get a ride from a gal who worked there part time, too. On the days I didn't work at Wal-Mart I could get a ride home with Bob. He sat next to me in some of my classes. He was from Chicago and had moved here just before I did. So we had something in common. When I told him where I was from, he made me show it to him on a map. When Bob would bring me home, Dad would take him right back to his gun collection. He taught Bob how to shoot and gave Bob a brief course on gun safety. Then we would blast the hell out of Dad's targets that were made of wooden planks in the back yard. Dad's influence on Bob would be with him all of his life. Bob took up the hobby and did his own reloading, later on in life. He got involved in the Bianchi Cup, and came in third place out of 400 plus shooters and got a beautiful plaque for his shooting abilities. He still talks about the time Dad put the 45-70 in his hands and let him shoot! That rifle was like a small cannon, and when Bob shot it, he about landed on his butt. I think he was addicted ever since. So to this day Bob has never forgotten the thrill he got from my dad's guns and the influence Dad left on him. Now Bob tries to influence the younger generation to do the same and went on to be a lifelong member of the NRA.

Now, we didn't have too many animals down here like at the other farmhouse up in PA. We brought the two horses, Joker and Flash, but there wasn't anywhere to ride them down here. The closest gravel road was about three miles away and there was no berm on the side of the black top roads. They drove too fast out here to ride the horses anywhere, so all I had was the pasture, which was a drag compared to what we had before. So the horses didn't get ridden too much, until I asked the local farmers who had pasture adjoining ours, if it was okay to ride in theirs, and it was cool with them. We also had the dogs. We started out with Hiedy, but she caught the mange and Dad couldn't get rid of it, so she disappeared one day. I don't know if the vet had her put down or he did it himself. And Gee, Gee whom I think died of old age. Then Dad ordered another St. Bernard out of a Sears' catalog. We had to go to the airport and pick her up. We had her for a few years, until I told Dad she looked sick. He said that she was supposed to look that way because St. Bernards have a sad looking face. But she wasn't eating and Dad took her to the vet and she got put down, supposedly. Then I found out there was a scam going on at the Vet's office with pedigree dogs. So I'm not sure what really happened to her. Then Tim wanted a dog and Dad got him a bigger St. Bernard. She didn't last too long because Tim thought that since she was a big dog he could take flying leaps and jump on her back and knock her down. I kept telling him that he was going to hurt her internally because she would yip every time he did it. One day she was dead out in the yard. He tried to blame it on a snakebite, but when I asked him where she was bit, (because some dogs are immune to venom), there was no evidence. I think it was because he roughhoused with her too much. He not only bullied other kids but he bullied our animals, too. Then Dad got Ruby a little Welsh terrier we named Sassy. Well, Tim ended up breaking that little dog's front leg from playing to hard with her. So she had a crooked leg thanks to him, because Dad didn't take her to the vet. So the only pets Tim had that he couldn't hurt was a turtle. He would go out and collect box turtles and Dad built a coral for them in the back yard so they couldn't get away. They started laying eggs everywhere so we let them go. I had a pet skunk for a summer. Roseanne went down in the pasture in the old barn and said there was a baby skunk down there, and came walking up with one holding it away from her by the tail. I took it and cuddled it and made a pet out of her until she was ready to leave. She only sprayed me once and that was when I took her from Roseanne and it just left a little stain on my shirt. I fed her cherries from our cherry tree and cat food. Then there was Becky, a Rottweiler that cousin Rich and Cindy gave Dad. He loved that dog. He would play the harmonica and taught her how to sing. The dog and he would be out on the front porch playing the harmonica and singing. But she had diabetes and Dad couldn't afford the insulin for her. She weighed over 130 pounds so she had to be put down. Sassy ended up getting to old to see and was running into walls, so when

Dad and Ruby went on vacation one year, Dad dug a hole and asked me
if I would take her to the vet to have her put down. So I did and buried
her in the hole Dad dug for a grave and put a little marker on it for her.
After that Rosella gave Ruby a goofy looking half-breed Weiner dog that
was not housetrained but was supposed to be. It finally died after staining
up the rugs. Then there was Midge, that was Dad's Weiner dog that he had
forever. So that took care of the dogs and we can't forget the Beagles. If they
didn't hunt rabbits, they would get buckshot coming their way. I remember
Dad and I going rabbit hunting one day with the two dogs. I could tell
them apart, the female had a white belly and Sam, the male was more black
and tan. Dad was calling them and the female would never come to him
and he would get mad. So he was off in the distance trying to get the dog to
come to him. All of a sudden I heard, "Bang" and Dad said he had taught
that dog a lesson because "she" wouldn't come to him. Well, I said, "Way
to go Dad, you shot the wrong dog." I had the female with me the whole
time: he had shot the good dog, "Sam". He started crying and cussing,
and when we got home, he called my sister Carol up and told her what
he did. She started laughing and told him, "That'll teach ya." So he wasn't
going to get any sympathy for what he did. One time I was looking down
into the pasture and saw something down there that looked like a big bird
of some kind, so I went down there to see what it was. It was some great
horned owl that couldn't fly. So I threw my jacket over it and brought it up
to the house. Dad and I made a place for it in the storage area behind the
garage. It sat on the perch and would click its beak together as a warning
that it would bite if we got close enough. Dad and I thought we could
nurse it back to health so every day I would go out there and feed it balls
of hamburger with a spoon. I guess someone had shot it with a shotgun,
probably because they had chickens or they were just cruel. I believe it died
from blood poisoning.

After working awhile at Wal-Mart, I came across a small 13 inch black
and white TV for my room. Since cable hadn't been invented yet, my little
TV would get in at least seven channels just with the antenna. I would sit
up in my room a lot and watch my little TV. It was a Sanyo and I couldn't
believe how well the picture would come in. It was the first TV I ever owned.
I paid $35 for it back then. I think it was a hot TV, But we won't dwell on
that. Anyway, things were going pretty good. I had a part time job and
going to school and all. One day Dad wanted to use my TV to watch at his
place of employment, working at night at the Capitol building. So I let him
use it. I would often go down and see Dad on the weekends at the clear well

down below the Capitol building. But one day I went down there and my TV was gone! "Where's my TV?" Dad said, "I broke it." So I asked, "What broke on it?" He said, "Everything." How could everything break on my TV? Apparently when you throw a small TV across the room and it hits a block wall things are going to tend to break and what exactly possessed him to do this you might ask? Well when we were kids we would always stay up late and watch horror flicks, like the Wolfman and Dracula, etc. Dad saw where Wolfman was in the TV guide late that night. So expecting to see Lon Chaney, Jr. appear on the screen as the Wolfman, he found out he waited up to see Wolfman Jack. Dad hated Wolfman Jack. He didn't want to watch "The Midnight Special" hosted by Wolfman Jack and there went my TV. I guess Dad didn't think to just turn it off. He did the same thing to a gas-powered airplane that I bought Tim for his birthday. We put it all together just so Dad could fly it into the side of the rock house we lived in. Tim never got to touch it. The plane didn't survive the crash.

Since we lived here for a little while, Dad decided we needed religion and would start going to church. So we started going to this little Pentecostal Church up the road. Dad always sang louder that anyone else did. He would always wait until we were in the middle of a song before he would pass gas. That way no one would hear it. But we all sure smelled it. I told him that one day God was going to get him for that, and sure enough, Dad farted and crapped down both his pant legs and had to leave. He left Tim and I to walk home. After we got home, I looked at Dad and said, "I told you God was going to get you for that. I don't think he went back to church after that. So Tim and I continued to go for a while. I never heard of people speaking in tongues before, but one day I was sitting next to this one guy that threw himself down on the floor and was speaking some foreign language. I looked at him and jumped outta the way. I didn't know what was going on. Then they asked him to translate. This took some getting used to, so I decided the youth group would be better for me to deal with. I continued to go for awhile until one day there was a guest speaker that came to preach to us from another state. He was collecting money for some charity. They must have passed the basket around five times for him. Tim and I didn't have any money to put in the basket, and when the speaker stood up and said, "Bless those who give and don't bless those that don't give", I took Tim and we walked home. We didn't have anything to give except ourselves. So we left and I don't remember ever going back. But shortly after, the church changed hands. I think it changed hands several times.

When I turned 18 Dad told me I could date, but there wasn't any boys interested in me. So I would often pal around with a girlfriend of mine. I would go over to her folk's house and spend the night. I'm not sure what was going on in Dad's head, but I was getting the impression that maybe he thought I was gay or something, since I was running around with girls instead of dating boys. If the boys had a car and asked me out, I would have considered it. But I had more fun with the girls. So he started telling me that the boys needed to come to the door and pick me up, or I wasn't going anywhere. Since I didn't know any boys that were willing to come pick me up my girlfriend's sister knew someone that would come to the door so I could get out of the house. The next thing I knew a Mustang was coming down the driveway. The person driving was supposed to be my date and my two friends were in the car squatting down so Dad didn't see them. Anyway, I didn't even know this guy's name or who the hell he even was, and after seeing him, I wasn't sure I wanted to know. He was a bearded dude with long shaggy black hair kind of resembling a sasquatch. As soon as he came to the door I ran out like a flash before Dad could say anything to him. When I got to the car to get in I saw my two friends in the car. One was in the front and one was in the back. He got in the driver's seat and I had to get in the back seat. I told the guy, "Just hurry up and get out of the driveway!" I think after that Dad didn't care if I was out with the girls.

About this time Dad's little truck he'd bought was needing some body work, so Chaz and Dad started patching it up with Bondo. It was a 58 Ford with a Six Banger in it and a geared up rear end. After the Bondo dried and the sanding was done Dad and I went outside with a roller and paintbrushes to give the little truck its new look. It was originally turquoise but since Dad had some left over red and black paint that's what colors it would be. We painted the front cab red and the truck bed was black. You could see the paint streaks in it from the brush, but above all, it didn't look too bad. Since we brushed the paint on it, it never rusted out after that. It was a fun truck to drive with the three on the tree.

Since Dad was in the painting mood, it was time for a few more home improvements. The upstairs bedroom windows needed scraped and painted. Tim's room was at the top of the stairs and my room was above the living room. There was no wall dividing the two rooms so I would tack a blanket up for privacy. While I climbed out the bedroom window to get started on my side Dad was sizing up the situation on Tim's side. Now at our house the bathroom was right at the base of the stairs so when Dad went over to Tim's side he was furious. He called Tim everything but a white boy. That stupid kid was so lazy that he was urinating out the window and had rotted all the woodwork around the windows. It smelt awful and to top it all off it was going into the well. I think Dad wanted to beat the crap out of him at that point and I was willing to help hold the little brat for him. He got by with an ass beating instead, and at that Ruby didn't have a whole lot to say about her precious son. She made up for it later, I'm sure. So Dad and I had to tear out the windows on his side and replace all the wood with Dad cussing all the way. After we got done with the windows Dad and I went to get some gas at a place called Apache Flats. We hopped in the ol' truck and headed on down there to one of the stores. Well on the way back it started to sprinkle out and when Dad turned the wipers on, they weren't wiping fast enough and would always get stuck. Since Dad had some extra rope in the back we could pull the wipers with, and keep them going. Apparently the hydraulics weren't working too good. But that's okay because the emergency break didn't work either, so Dad rigged up a wedge shaped block of wood, with a small chain attached to throw behind the tire in case he had to park on a hill. Believe it or not it worked. This technique would be known as "Brown technology" after his name.

Since we had both the truck and the car, sometimes Roseanne and Chaz would hop in the wagon with us and go to the store just up the road. They had a blue 1970 Ford pick up truck and when it rained they would borrow the wagon. Well one day dad and I were headed for the grocery store and stopped at Roseanne and Chaz's to see if there was anything they needed, so Chaz hopped in with Dad and I and we were off. But as soon as we headed down the road a doe jumped out in the road and Dad hit it. So we turned around and loaded it up in the back of the wagon, (we folded the back seat down), and headed back to their house to hang it up in the tree in their front yard. On the way Dad looked in the rear view mirror and we freaked out because the deer was standing up all sprawled out in the back of the station wagon. We pulled into the yard and as we walked around the back of the wagon the deer was trying to jump out. Chaz grabbed it and started punching on its head. The deer was using its front hooves to defend itself and was beating the crap out of Chaz, while Dad was trying to tackle it down from the rear. Dad was screaming, "Get a gun, get a gun!" So I ran in the house and told Roseanne to get me a gun, that Dad and Chaz were fighting a deer in the wagon. She came out with a pistol and was yelling, "Don't hurt it, don't hurt it!" All the time Chaz was bloodied up from the deer kicking the crap out of him. Dad grabbed the gun and shot the deer in the station wagon! I screamed, "Oh my God!"

Then we put the tailgate down and drug the doe out of the station wagon and told Roseanne, "Here's your damn groceries!" After we got the deer hung up in the front yard, Dad and Chaz were comparing their injuries. Chaz's hand was all swollen up and he couldn't believe how hard that deer's head was. Apparently Dad just knocked it out when he hit it with the car, and it was not a happy deer when it woke up. So while they skinned it out, I cleaned the wagon up.

At one other time there was a contest at Wal-Mart. It was a local fishing tournament sponsored by the store. Well Dad and Chaz decided to go fishing at Binder Lake one day. They couldn't catch anything and were about to give up, when Chaz snagged something big on his line. It was a big bass! After getting it reeled in they realized that the fish had been caught once before and must have escaped somehow because of the rope tied through the gills and out of the mouth. Chaz's hook was just in the right place at the right time! So after catching the bass they were excited about showing it to everyone at home. That's when someone told them about the fishing tournament. Since it was Sunday, Dad and Chaz knew that they had to keep the fish alive all night to enter it the next morning at Wal-Mart. Dad suggested we put the fish in the bathtub and baby-sit it all night. So as a good sport, I decided to help out by moving the fish back and forth to keep the oxygen moving through its gills. So all the time Dad and I stayed up with the fish we would laugh and splash water on each other and play with the stupid fish, (that didn't' look like it was going to make it to me). Dad would say, "Wouldn't that be the shits if the contest was already over and we sat up all night for nothing." Oh well, it's not the worst thing we ever did, and besides were having fun. So the next morning while the fish was barely hanging on, Chaz came over and Dad and he took the fish into Wal-Mart Monday morning. Dad said everyone was staring at them in Wal-Mart as they carried their prize to the back of the store. Of course Dad and Chaz thought they were just looking at the fish, when in fact, the contest deadline was over a week ago and the judging was last week already. So after embarrassing themselves and getting a good laugh out of it, they brought the fish home. Dad took its head and nailed to the garage wall so he could tell everyone about his big adventure. Yes, the fish head did stink for sometime until it finally dried out. Then he painted varnish on it to give it that wet look. Only Dad would have done something like that, but it was a trophy!

Roseanne and Chaz didn't live in Missouri very long. They rented a couple of houses close by but got into some financial problems and ended up moving to Texas. Soon I would be graduating from school. Dad made me ride the bus until I graduated. After graduating in May, Dad took me around to all the local factories and I was offered a job between Cheeseborough-Ponds (they made cosmetics) or Westinghouse, (they made underground transformers). I would be working the night shift so Dad could take me back and forth to work. After taking a tour of both shops, I ended up choosing the cosmetic factory because it was cleaner, and it was right on the way to the maintenance building Dad worked in for the state capitol. So as Dad and I rode together to work every day, I managed to save enough money to buy my first car. Of course Dad wouldn't let me buy any of the cars I wanted, so I settled for a 1964 Ford Custom 500 (4 door hardtop). It was a far cry from the 1969 Chevelle with a 396 V-8 that I wanted. But I guess Dad knew I would be hot-rodding it, so I got the Ford with the little 260 V-8 in it. So I couldn't wait to get my driver's permit so Dad could go out with me and drive it We had it inspected and licensed, and I was ready to go, so I thought. While the permits came and went, Dad wouldn't come out with me so I could drive it. He never even sat in it with me. It was obvious that Dad didn't want me going anywhere and was afraid he would lose control of my life. So one morning after Dad brought me home, I was tired as usual and went on up to bed, only to be woken up by Ruby and Dad's constant arguing. I overheard Ruby calling me a whore because I was out all night. So I came downstairs to confront her and let her know that I was working in a shop all night and besides, Dad was taking me to work. Well, we got into it in the kitchen, and when she raised her hand to slap me, I raised my fist to punch her and at that time Dad grabbed both of us. I went flying into the living room on the couch and Ruby got shoved into the area that Dad put an addition on, which was the dining area. So I went out on the front porch and sat there. Pretty soon Dad came out and told me that Ruby was going through menopause. Every time Dad tried to correct Tim, Ruby would take it out on me. So I told Dad I was moving out, even though I didn't have a driver's license, I backed my car up to the front porch and proceeded to throw my clothes into the trunk. Well, Dad wasn't happy about this and tried to bluff me into staying by telling me, "If you leave, don't come back." I left home believing my dad didn't want me around anymore. I had my car and my clothes and went and stayed with my girlfriend's folks, and bought them groceries every week for room and board. About six months went by without seeing or hearing from anyone. I didn't call because I figured they all got what they wanted. I know Ruby and Little Brother were happy anyway. But I wasn't and with no guidance I found myself in some strange predicaments. Trying to sleep during the day in someone else's house wasn't working out. Since I didn't have any car insurance when I got side swiped by a drunk on the way to work one night I couldn't report it and had to drive my car around with the side bashed in. Then my friends' sister was jealous of me and she kept vandalizing my car. I was having to replace the radiator, all the caps under the hood, the gas tank and this was beginning to be an issue. So I knew I couldn't stay with her folks anymore. At the same time I happened to run into my stepbrother, Ross, Who was divorced and was staying here temporarily. He told me that Dad was worried about me and regretted my leaving. So I went home to see Dad; to see if he still loved me. He hugged me and we hashed things out. He knew Ruby and I weren't going to get along so he told me of a trailer for rent a friend of his had in their back yard that was just up the road. So a girlfriend and I moved in it to share expenses. My Dad's friend's name was Brooks. After living there for a while things weren't working out between my roommate and me. She turned out to be a major slob and brought cockroaches in with her belongings. Plus Brooks adopted a stray German Shepherd that wouldn't let us out of the trailer. One day I went out to check the mail and the dog attacked me. He went for my throat, but I put my arm up and he bit my arm. So I grabbed him by the jaws and backed him up into a shed, closed the door and ran like hell to the trailer and called Dad and told him what had been going on with this dog. So here comes Dad to the rescue. He got out of his truck and had a club in his hand. When the dog came after Dad that dog got the crap clubbed out of him and went yipping back to the house. After Dad and Brooks had a few words I knew that I wasn't going to live there very long because Brooks wasn't going to get rid of the dog. So shortly after Dad told Brooks to go hammer his ass, (which was one of Dad's favorite sayings) and I was getting laid off from work anyway. I ended up moving back home for a while. So I sold my Ford, which was on its last leg anyway, and just knowing how that was going to make Ruby feel, I decided to go up north to PA and stay with my sister and draw unemployment up there for a while. I stayed with my sister for awhile but was soon called back to work. I went back home and Dad and I went to look for me another clunker to drive. I ended up getting a 1963 Chevy impala that only ran on 7 cylinders. After being back at work I let Dad's friend rebuild the engine. After spending $500 to have that done it still didn't run worth a damn, but it got me around. One day I got it stuck in the mud and a friend of mine tried to push it out and couldn't. I put it in low and then in reverse while he tried to push it. So I let him try to drive it out and he kept his foot on the gas will slamming it in gears and ruined the transmission in it. One day I was going to the store and had to pull over into a gravel pit, the transmission went completely out of it. We had to let it set there for a couple of days before we could haul it off to be fixed and one day Dad was driving by and saw someone in my car! He pulled up behind it to see what the guy was doing. He was stealing my radio! Dad asked him if he needed any help and he said, "No, I think I got it." So Dad said, as he went to the front of my car, "Hey, I think you better come over here and look at this," pointing to the bumper. When the guy took himself out from under the dash of my car to look where Dad was pointing, Dad gave him an uppercut to his jaw and practically broke the guy's face. He told him that this was his daughter's car and to get the hell out of there. The guy staggered back to his vehicle with his bloody face and drove off. Shortly after that we got my car fixed and were off cruisin' again.

It was getting to be wintertime again. Ross was offered a job in Arizona, where he met a girl with two kids and they were married. Dad and I started cutting and splitting wood for winter. It was a good way to avoid Ruby, since her attitude hadn't improved any. Tim's nasty name-calling and tattle telling showed no improvements either. But the holidays were rolling around and we always had a house full. Every holiday my sisters and their kids would come to Missouri and we always had a good time together. Dad always kept us all together even if they lived out of state. Except Shelly, she only came down one time in 30 years. The more of us there was, the merrier. As usual we would do anything for a laugh. Ruby had some really stringy short hair and somehow she had acquired this goofy looking wig. Dad and all of us used to come out with it on and act stupid with it. You would have sworn we had never seen a wig before. After we had all made fun with it, I don't remember seeing the wig anymore. Dad started taking Ruby out to get perms after that. We would get the horses saddled and go riding and show the grandkids how to ride when everyone was here. There was always someone passing through Missouri and going up to Pennsylvania. So Dad's place was a good place for Roseanne and Chaz, or Molly and her family to stop at. Carol and Rosella would often come down to visit, too.

But in the meantime I still had to look for another place to live. One day I heard of a trailer that the local bank had for sale. It was a takeover payment deal, so I signed the papers and took over the payments. Since my girlfriend's dad owned a trailer park, he helped me move the trailer and get it set up. Dad came out and we set up a wood stove in it because it had an oil-burning furnace that wasn't in too good of shape. We helped each other out in the wintertime.

In the meantime I had my girlfriend and her boyfriend move in with me because they had nowhere to stay. They stayed for a while until she moved to Mississippi, leaving him there. He had a fawn colored Doberman Pincher name Zeke. Well we asked Dad to dog sit Zeke one time for us and he agreed. Well Zeke had never seen a chicken before and Ruby had Ducks and chickens. When Davis and I went to Ohio where he was from for a visit, Zeke got into the chicken coop. Dad wasn't mad about it because he was supposed to be watching the dog. When we got back home I noticed one of the hens was pecking the ground kinda funny. Dad and I caught it and saw that it had a big cut in its neck. She was a victim of the dog. Dad and I got a needle and thread and while I stretched the chicken's neck out, Dad took to sewing it. The least he could have done was sew it together straight. But he didn't and although the chicken lived, its head was all cock-eyed from its skin getting stitched up very crooked. But the damn thing could still eat so we didn't worry about it too much. But after looking at all of the rest of the chickens, Zeke had plucked all the rest of those chickens bald. He would grab them by their tail feathers and so Ruby's chickens ran around all year with what we started calling a special breed of "baldass" chickens.

Davis and I had an off and on relationship for about 12 years. In that amount of time I managed to save up enough money to buy me a three-wheeler. It was a 1965 Police Special, with a 45 flathead motor. It would cruise 60 miles an hour with a good tailwind. I guess meter maids weren't supposed to go fast, but it was a Harley and Dad sure did like it. I liked it too, but it was too slow, and I ended up selling it and having a two wheeler built. But that was okay, because Dad liked it also. Just so it was a Harley, because Dad had one that he rode that had a sidecar attached. Apparently a friend and he tried driving it through two trees and wrecked it. That was long before I was even thought of. But I always rode my bike to Dads. He liked hearing it run. So anyway when I bought my first Harley Dad came right out and we built a shed in the back of the trailer and put a lock on it. It had a kennel attached to the back so my dog could run in and out. There were a couple of times when I was out partying with my friends and it would be late, Dad would be at work in the clear well below the capitol building. So we would go over there and visit him. He was always happy for the company. When my party buddies and I came to the capitol maintenance shop down from the capitol Dad would give us midnight tours. We got to go up in the whispering tower and ride the governors' elevator. It was a thrill to go up into the dome and look at all the stucco and insulation that was sprayed inside the walls. All we had to walk on was some wooden planks. We could come out right under the lady at the top of the capitol building, (I think she's the goddess of grain). Anyway the concrete walls up there were at least 2 and ½ feet thick. Dad wouldn't go up with us because he was afraid of heights. We made sure to go up and come right back down so he wouldn't get in any kind of trouble. On the way back down we could read the graffiti that was written on the inside of the dome. Some of it was dated back to the 1960's when they used to give tours in there. It was an experience that they, (my friends), would never forget, since they lived here all their lives and never got the opportunity to check it out before. As we left the building Dad took us through the tunnel, connecting the maintenance building (clear well) to the basement of the capitol. We all told Dad how grateful we were. After we all thanked him, I hugged him and we left, ending our night with a great experience.

Dad and Ruby would often come out to my trailer when Tim was in school. I can remember buying a 1950 Cadillac that I wanted to fix up sometime in the future. I had the idea, but knew nothing about the know how. But it was neat, and educational, learning about that style of automobile. Dad liked old cars, and just getting our pictures taken with it was cool enough. But it was complete and did run, but the brakes were weak and there was something going on with the hydraulics that I wasn't sure about. I didn't want to go down the road having to pull any ropes through the windows or use a block of wood for an emergency break, so I just sat on it in hopes that I could get it running someday. But anyway Dad brought Tim with him one time. I had a dog in the front yard and one in the back yard. My German Shepherd was in the back where my bike was, and my Pit Bull Doberman mix was in the front chained up. He was like my doorbell you might say. He was a big husky dog, and the rougher someone would play with him, the rougher he would play back. Well, Tim was out there doing something with the dog while Dad and I were in the trailer doing something with the woodstove. I know he was out there playing with the dog. After Tim and Dad left and I saw my dog limping on his front paw. I knew Tim was going to be up to no good. I swear that kid had it out for me. Anyway I looked at my dog's leg and he yipped. (His name was Spit.) So I gave them time to get back home and I got Dad on the phone and told him that Tim had hurt my dog. Of course,

Tim denied everything and said that he didn't do anything to my stupid dog. So I'm sure Dad let him know that we weren't proud of the way he treated animals. But Spit healed up okay. The other dog, Zeke the chicken plucker, got shot by some kids with a 22 caliber rifle. His leg got shot in half and after some difficulty he had after having a plate put in his leg to hold it together, he caught pneumonia and died in the doghouse.

At about this time my sister Carol would be coming down and spending some time in Missouri. She had broken her thumb and was on medical leave from the furniture factory in Pennsylvania. Now since my sister was born on April Fool's Day, Dad and I liked messing with her head a little. We were always telling her stories to see if she would believe us. So one day we needed to go to the store at Apache Flats. It was just an old strip of highway that consisted of a few gas stations, a mini-mart and a store called The House of Bargains, which had a little bit of everything in it, but definitely not any Indians. So we asked Carol if she wanted to go with us to Apache Flats. When she asked what was down there, well, Dad and I came up with a story that would have even made the Indians proud, if there would have been any. Dad started telling her of a tribe of Indians living down there on a reservation that made their money selling souvenirs, and how they lived in teepees, and how the government took their land away and just did them so wrong. She was just feeling so sorry for those Indians at Apache Flats. We thought she was going to break out a prayer and start praying for them right there in the truck, them poor Indians. Then we pulled into the mini-mart and she asked how far it was to the reservation and I know we shouldn't have done it, but she was so easy that she would believe everything we told her. Anyway we confessed that were no Indians at the flats and then she didn't believe we could have made that up driving all the way back from there. Once Dad and I got started fooling Carol, there was no stopping us. Dad had a year to think of what pranks he was going to pull on her every time her birthday or just every occasion rolled around. She always took it well and knew he was just funnin'.

Soon it was time for little brother to graduate. Since he was going to graduate in May and his birthday was in June, Tim decided to join the Navy. He thought that if he would join the Navy that Dad would be proud of him. So Dad had a combination, graduation, birthday and bon voyage party for him. Dad got the barbecue going and we had a small get together to see Momma's little baby off. Things were actually going pretty good for all of us at that time. Ruby had a whole different attitude with me and Dad and she weren't arguing and things started running like a well-oiled machine. I would pick Ruby up and we would go shopping and have a good time, since Dad didn't like getting out and going shopping. Besides, we were starting to get closer and she started seeing me as more of an asset, without little brother manipulating everything. Things were going good for us and Dad would take me with them and we would go out and eat and go to some second hand stores, etc. Everyone was getting along. Well in less than a year later, Tim was coming home on leave with the girl he wanted to marry. I knew the girl was pregnant, just by looking at her. She was the first one he had ever been with and she already had another child and had been married before. When I asked him if he had to marry her, he lied to us. I could tell that there was trouble before he even told us that they wanted to get married. She was more experienced than he was, and she took him, hook, line and sinker. They ended up having a little girl that ended up with my sister Molly because Tim's new wife left him and the baby, while he was out on the submarine. So Molly and her family gave the little girl all the love they could. They would often come to Missouri to visit Granma and Grampa. The little girl would be taught good family values and Molly was ready to adopt her, but then Tim didn't like that idea and got a discharge from the Navy and took his daughter back. Everyone knew the girl was better off with Molly, but that's another story. So Tim came home and lived in a trailer park with his little girl and Ross divorced his second wife and moved to Missouri to work for the state.

Through the years I continued going over to Dad's and we were both still working nights. I would sew all of their clothes that needed mending and take Ruby grocery shopping. Dad was changing too. He was encouraging Ruby to buy whatever she wanted, so we would hit the jewelry stores and go to the malls. We would kid around about Dad and on the holidays he would barbecue his chicken and pork steaks for everyone who came out. Life was good.

At about this time, I had met someone else through my friend Bob and his wife. After living in my little trailer for twelve years, it was time to move out and start a new life. I moved in with John. He had his own house in Holts Summit. He wanted the country life and so did I. We both had good jobs and I went to day shift. But I was always going back home and keeping in touch with Dad and Ruby. Ross and his 3rd wife lived close by in Holts Summit, too. One year we went to Ross's for Christmas. It was a nice gathering until I saw my mom's nativity scene on their television set. I was devastated to see it in the hands of people that didn't have a clue as to what kind of meaning it would have for Carol or I. To see them with what was under my mom's tree as we were growing up just broke my heart. When I asked them where they had gotten it, I found out my dad gave it to them. I was blown away. Nobody else should have gotten that but Carol or me, since we didn't get anything when our mom died. That nativity was precious to us. So after John and I got back home I was bawling my eyes out for three days. When I went over to Dad's to confront him about it, I could hardly talk because I was so upset. Ross was not going to get anything that belonged to my mom if I could help it. Finally I asked him, while I held back the tears, "Why does Ross and Bev have my mom's nativity set? It doesn't mean anything to them." Ruby yelled out, "I told you not to give that to them." So Dad told me he would get it back after Christmas . . . and give it to Carol! Well, that upset me again. Here I was the one fighting for it, and he wants to give it to my sister up in PA when I'm right here. So I called Carol on up and let her know what was going on. She thought I should have it and so dad gave the nativity scene to me, which had been in our family for over fifty years. I put it up in a special place every Christmas to celebrate the birth of our Lord, Jesus, and the memory of our mom.

Since John and I now lived together, we were thinking of our future and the motorcycles, (he had a Harley, too), would be getting sold. We lived out on 2.5 miles of gravel road and it wasn't good for the bikes to have to get all dusty and beat up on. So we sold them, and put up some pasture to raise a couple of beef on. Dad was happy to help. We bought a meat saw and grinder, and would have a spot in our garage to butcher anything that we had including deer. But I'm getting a little ahead of myself here.

To go back to where I was; John and I started living together. We were together for four years before we tied the knot. Dad was more than eager to give me away. We were married in a pavilion at one of the city parks. Everyone but Shelly made it. My sister Carol was my bridesmaid. We tried to keep it simple, but a year before we got married I had taken a bad spill at work and was on a medical leave. A year later they sent me a "Dear John" letter, terminating my employment, but it didn't stop us.

Anyway since I was home all the time, I decided to take up a hobby; taxidermy. Since we had always done our own meat processing, I knew I could handle the squeamish parts of it. Dad was thrilled to help participate by picking up some road kill for me to experiment with. Some of it was not very fresh either. I always told him to look at the eyes of the varmint before he picked it up. He called me up and told me about a mother coon and three babies he had found on the road. He assured me that . . . "They were fresh". So I told him to put them in a garbage bag and put them in the freezer and we would be there to pick them up at the house. John and I headed out to Dad's with a cooler and put the raccoons in it and headed back to the house. We got half way home and smelled something real bad coming from the cooler. We pulled over and dumped those coons out on the side of the road. They were very far from being a fresh road kill. So I encouraged Dad to not pick anything up off the road for me after that. After doing taxidermy as a hobby, I decided to do it as a business. I would do everything but the painting. John seemed to have the knack for that. Dad loved seeing the big bucks that were brought in and would help me in the mounting process. He would help me stretch the hides and put them on the mannequins, and would sit there all day with me while I created works of art out of a lifeless piece of skin. Every time the boys would go out deer hunting, Dad would scarf up the feet and tails to make thermometers and other things out of for Christmas gifts and birthdays. He was always putting in an order for that sort of stuff.

One year deer season rolled around and I wanted to go. John, my two brothers and Dad were always going, but I never got to go. It was a man thing. So one day I sat out in the rain all day behind the house on the eight acres we had, and saw nothing. I guess Ross and John felt bad about it and snuck me in where they went hunting. Tim and Dad didn't know I was out there on the 60+ acres they were hunting on, and sure enough, here came a buck up the gully. I got so nervous that I couldn't steady my gun for a shot. As I was sitting on a stump, I put my elbows on each knee, and while I was turned sideways, I took a shot. The buck jumped up and took a big kick and took off! I didn't know where he went! I looked for a blood trail, but there wasn't any. So I went looking for it and got lost, but managed to find my way back to my stump. Along the way I saw a doe. I wasn't going to shoot at her because I had already lost one deer and wasn't going to shoot another. When I finally made it back, I sat there; and I'll be damned if another buck wasn't coming up right behind me. So as he slowly walked by, he went down into a gully and I put the scope on him, a leaf started dangling in front of my scope and I couldn't get a shot off at him. I went back and sat down, and thought of how stressful this deer hunting could be. Soon after that Ross came over and we looked for my deer but never found it. Tim was telling me I missed. After telling Dad what the deer did when I shot it, he and the guy who owned the land, went back over and looked for it and found it. The buck had circled right behind me and laid down with his legs tucked under him, so we couldn't see his white belly. When

Dad called I was hysterically happy and almost blew his eardrums out over the phone. I had earned my dad's respect and he was proud of me every time we would go out hunting together.

I guess things weren't going too well in Ross's third marriage either. He and wife number three were getting a divorce, but Tim was getting married. Tim and Jeana got married at church close by Dad's house. It was the only wedding where the bride came down the aisle to the tune of "Amazing Grace". I had always thought of that as being something we sang at funerals, but it was their wedding, so several of us kept our mouths shut. Not long after that they had their first baby and Cassey would have a little brother. The only reason I'm writing about this is because it always leads into something else.

It turned out Molly's oldest daughter was getting married in Louisiana. We were all making plans to go down to the wedding. Tim and his family would be following John and I down to Shreveport. Dad and Ruby would go down in their van that Dad bought recently. We camped out all the way down through Arkansas. It wasn't too bad on the way down and we would all stay in a rental house that Molly and her second husband owned. Tim and Jeana totally trashed their room, while we kept our room clean and neat. We kept Tim's room's door closed because of the dirty diapers thrown everywhere. They had no respect for the free room and board that they were getting. Dad was always fighting with everyone over the remote control for the TV. Then at the wedding, which was in a beautiful rose garden, a damn bird crapped on my outfit. I had to change my clothes because I had a big stain on my shoulder. After the wedding was over Dad washed himself up in Molly's swimming pool with a bar of soap. He obviously had no idea how much chemicals cost to keep the pool water clean. All I thought was, "I'll bet they'll be glad when everyone's out of here."

John and I decided to follow Dad back home. We had enough of Tim and his family for a while. That's when we realized just how bad Dad's driving had gotten. He was all over the road. He pulled out in front of semi tractor-trailer rigs and didn't even look out his mirrors before he passed anyone. When we hit a storm and had to pull over because we couldn't see where the hell we were going, Dad would forget to put the van up in park. The next thing we knew the van was starting to back up into our Bronco. John laid on the horn as we were trying to prevent Dad from backing up into us. Since there weren't any cell phones back then, communicating with Dad was almost impossible. After we were back on the road we had to race up next to him and practically force him to pull over or stop somewhere.

Coming up through Arkansas following Dad was nerve racking. We wanted to stop for food and a bathroom break. John and I wanted some barbecue and saw a place we could stop at. Dad came into the restaurant behind us. At this time we were all tired and hungry from driving and wanted to eat and get a motel room. But Dad didn't like the restaurant because they had serving size portions. It wasn't an all you could eat place. He proceeded to have a fit, which embarrassed us. So I told him to just go eat where he wanted. After he left the guy behind the counter gave John and I an extra helping of potato salad for getting Dad out of his eating establishment. After that John and I would start taking Ruby and Dad with us to the state fairs, Indian pow-wows, the Ozark Extravaganza, some blue grass festivals and whatever else was going on in Missouri. We took them to places we thought they would enjoy, and we wouldn't have to worry about getting there in one piece. We had a good time anyway.

After that little trip was finally over, it was about time to start planning for Ruby and Dad's 25th wedding anniversary. We all agreed to have it up in Pennsylvania, because all of the family was up there, like Dad sisters, nieces, nephews, and my sister's families. It would be something nice for the rest of the family to do for them. We all went in on a silver 25th anniversary tray and had all our names put on it. It was really nice for them. They got to walk down the aisle again and renew their wedding vows and open gifts. They had a good time and even managed to make it back in one piece. After they made it back home from Pennsylvania we decided to go to the fair since it would be starting shortly.

When we went to the State Fair, Dad would always head for the pork house and we would order a big platter of spare ribs, and go watch the draft horse pulls. Dad and I would get excited and we would get to cheering for the teams as they were about to pull the sled. Ruby would always want us to keep quiet, but that wasn't going to happen. There was a team of big white geldings there that were getting ready to pull, but one of the horses couldn't pull for some reason. Another farmer lent the owner of the geldings one of his mares so he could stay in the competition. She was a much smaller horse and didn't have any shoes on her. The first thing my dad said was, "That mare will out pull that gelding." Sure enough when she heard that hook drop into that sled that little mare dropped to her knees and gave it all she had. The crowd was going nuts! She was pulling hard, as if her life depended on it. After she and that lazy gelding were unhooked the announcer told the guy that maybe he should get rid of the geldings and get him a pair of mares. Even if she wasn't shoed, she did a better job pulling. So Dad was excited and said, "See, I told ya so!" He was right! Also that day they had an Indian Pow Wow going on at the fair. I don't think my dad ever went to one of these before. As the Indians were in their costumes dancing and the drums were pounding, Dad jumped up off the bleachers and went down there in the middle of them and wanted them to stop so he could take pictures! I almost died laughing, at the look on all these Indians' faces in the middle of the ring performing their tribal dances. But they took it really well and were proud to get their pictures taken by this crazy pale face, that wasn't going to get out of the show until he got his pictures. It was never a dull moment around Dad. After that we would hit the air-conditioned arena to see what was going on in there. One time they were giving elephant rides and Dad paid for Ruby to ride the elephant. It was fun and she had a good time riding and feeding the huge animal. Since they had a chimpanzee out in the hallway she got her picture taken with it, too. But the biggest thrill my Dad got when we went to the fair was the draft horse hitches. This was totally awesome. The horses would be decked out in all kinds of fancy harnesses and pulling a fancy carriage or wagons. They would always start out with a single team (two horses) and eventually come out with a six-horse hitch team that would blow us away as they came into the arena at a full trot. They would fit at least ten teams in the arena at the same time. Ruby and Dad and I would be just going nuts. Dad would always want to jump over the rails and let the big horses just run over him, that's how excited he would get. Then there would be a grand finale. One time there was a stagecoach that had six or eight leopard appaloosa horses pulling it around the arena as fast as they could. The stagecoach was on two wheels every time they would round the end of the arena. I kept thinking that they were going to tip over. After the fourth or fifth time around, sure enough, over they went! As soon as those horses felt that coach go over they came to a complete stop. The two men on top just flew off in slow motion, got back up, flipped the stagecoach back over, climbed up it and gimped away. I don't think they ever came back. But it was exciting, and as I looked over at Dad he was in shock! His face was white and blank and we had to assure him that everyone was okay. But as I look back on our trips to the State Fair, when it came to horseflesh, Dad was never wrong. We could always pick the winners. Maybe we should have watched some horse racing, we could have won a buck or two maybe.

Another place we made a habit of going to every year was the Ozark Mountain Extravaganza, which was held at the Vichy Airport in Rolla. They had everything going on there; music, Civil War reenactments, good food, all the car parts, arts and crafts, new and used stuff, player pianos, and even the Keystone Cops and buggy rides. You name it and they probably had it, including Donna Douglas from the Beverly Hillbillies was there in her Ellie May outfit. She would walk around with the crowd and give a whistle every now and then. Dad would always carry his harmonica with him. One time he was invited to play it in a band that was there. It just made his day. We would always have to go back a second time just to look at everything. Even if there wasn't anything going on, I would go over to Dad's and putter around the house doing something, like working on his truck or doing some wood working projects. But Dad ended up giving the old 58 Ford to Ross. When he and Bev were divorced, Ross took to living in the bars. He wrecked about every automobile he ever had, including Dad's truck. I sure missed that truck. We had some good times in it. But dad got him another one. I think it was a 1978 Ford half ton. It was a pretty good truck. It had a V-8 under the hood, and of course a three on the tree. I was amazed at the fact that the windshield wipers worked and so did the emergency break. No more pulling strings or throwing a block of wood behind the tires. Damn, he was right up town, now!

Since Ruby and Dad were doing pretty good financially and Dad always wanted to help people who were less fortunate than us, Dad decided to adopt, (through the mail), a little boy named Anthony Tommy from an Indian reservation out West. They would write to Dad and tell him what Anthony needed for school and other things. If he needed shoes then Dad would send enough money to help him. The caseworkers would always send Dad progress reports. I think his mom was too poor to take care of him and his dad was an alcoholic. But through the years Anthony grew up and graduated from high school and it gave my dad a good feeling that his money was going to make a small boy's life better. Dad was awarded with a certificate of thanks and a letter from Anthony Tommy for the care packages and all the help he gave him through the years with the donations he would always send. Dad would keep Anthony's picture on the wall in the house for a long time until after he graduated.

At about this time Rosella and John would win four million dollars from the Pennsylvania Lotto. I remember the day Rosella called Dad up and told him all about it. Since Dad had a generous heart, I guess he thought Rosella and John would have one too. After Dad was done talking to them on the phone we were all under the impression that Rosella and John was going to share some of their fortune with us. Especially, since they were always poor as hell, and often had to borrow money from some of us. One time they came down to Missouri and their car quit on them. So I spent $250 on a car to get them back home. I never got repaid. Dad thought he had them convinced to give us at least $5000 a piece, but they were only telling Dad what he wanted to hear. Rosella and John made up for it in other ways. The money would have been nice though. John would go on hunting trips out West and they would travel around and visit everyone.

After dabbling in the taxidermy hobby for a while, I decided to try and make a go at it as a business. I practiced on the deer that we shot, so when the time came to take in some customers, I would know what to do. My buck was the first deer shoulder mount that I did. Rosella's husband donated a cape and some shed antlers from the hunts he went on. We were busy every season. I spent most of the time up in the garage skinning out deer capes and cutting the antlers off the skulls and record keeping. Dad always came out to look at the racks. Some of them were very nice bucks. It was always the trapping and hunting season that kept me the busiest. Dad was always ready to help participate in the occasion. He would always help me stretch the hides and would sit there for hours watching me put those deer together. There was a doe cape in the freezer that Dad had shot and I decided to put her together, too. One day Dad came out and saw the doe put together, drying on the wall and just fell in love with it. He kept trying to take her off the wall and sneak out of the house with her. I would have to yell at him and have him bring her back. One time he about cried because I wouldn't let him take her home. So I thought that year when Christmas rolled around that I would give it to him as a gift. I put a ribbon around its neck and gave her to him. He was so happy and knew right where he was going to hang her.

Since we had a meat saw and were planning on doing our own meat processing, we decided to cut up people's deer for them for a few extra dollars. After deer season was over, it was time for another job that we would get together for. Every year John and I would go buy a feeder calf at the Livestock Auction in the spring, fatten it up and process it. Usually we would buy two of them so everyone had a share of meat in their freezer. We didn't mind sharing. Now butchering hogs and beef was right up Dad's alley. It was something we always did years ago, so we cleaned the garage up, got the meat saw cleaned, and made room for our harvest time. Ross and Dad were always there and one year John's brother helped us. First we would lure the cattle to the feed trough. We would always turn it to where they would face down hill. Then John would go out there with the 22 rifle and shoot them in the head. As soon as they dropped, he would jump on them while they were still kicking and slice the jugular vein and they would bleed out on the spot. I know it sounds cruel, but that's how it's done. Then we would chain them to our tractor and drag them into the garage. Now this always happened in the coldest days of winter, like around January. That way we could leave them hanging for a couple of weeks, since we didn't have a walk-in freezer. After we dressed them out and they hung a while then it was time for the processing. I always had hot coffee and took an electric grill up there so we could carve and cook some fresh meat and have something hot to drink. We could take our time and have fun doing it. We would have a regular assembly line going. We would cut off a hunk of meat and cut steaks, roasts, and cut the fat off and run meat through the grinder for hamburger. John took to the butchering real good. He ran the meat saw and kept it clean and adjusted the blade when necessary. I did the labeling and wrapping. When we were through, everyone had enough meat to last them a long time. Even Tim, (who never once helped with the deer or meat processing), got to take some home from Dad's freezer. He never had to help us with any of the work, but he was always there to help himself to it. We even bought a pig, (250 pound hog), from a friend of John's, and processed it. We shot it right in the back of the truck. Now we did have a little trouble with Dad on that one. We had to clean and scrub the pig before we could take it into the garage. Dad had a problem with washing the pig crap off of him. So I had to keep reminding him that there was a bucket of hot soapy water there to keep his hands and knife clean. After we got done skinning and hanging that hog, John and I had to go back up and carve off some of the fat that had pig do-do on it. Maybe Dad didn't care about that but we did. Nevertheless, it came out all right. Dad did do the nastiest part, so it wasn't anything we couldn't take care of. It was always around a cold spell when we did this sort of thing. But one year we didn't need to do any processing, so Ruby and Dad decided to take a trip down South one year to visit my sisters, Roseanne in Texas and Molly in Louisiana. That meant someone had to take care of the two horses that Dad still had. Since it was wintertime, Dad assured me that Tim would make sure they were fed and watered, because there was no grass for them to eat and their water froze up all the time. He only lived about five miles from Dad's and I lived about 25 miles from Dad's. Well, I should have known not to trust Tim. He never liked the animals anyway, (or anything else for that matter), so I didn't go and check on them. I'll be damned if he didn't let those horses starve. Joker was already dead down in the pasture and Flash was skin and bones. I immediately called our vet and had him come over to Dad's and check Flash out so we could save her. I couldn't believe that Dad wouldn't even let the vet out of his truck. I had to tell Dad over and over again that John and I were paying for it before he finally let him see the horse. I had to put my foot down and insist that our vet saw the horse. After giving Flash a once over, he injected her with some vitamins and wormed her with the understanding that Dad would give her the rest of the worm medicine in a month. Well about five months later Flash was found on the hillside dead. She had kicked the spot out all around her, where she tried to get up. Both of the horses were over 30 years old. I was pretty upset with Dad when I found the worm medicine that he was supposed to give her on a shelf in the basement. But it probably wouldn't have helped her anyway. She was too far-gone, thanks to Tim. We sure did have a good time on those horses. Flash was the best horse we ever had, and Joker lived up to his name. He was always getting into trouble. Dad would always let them loose in the yard, and Joker would raid the chicken coop or we would have to chase him off the front porch. We would be sitting in the living room and Joker would be looking at us through the window. After the horses died, John had a friend up the street from Dad that had a backhoe. He was kind enough to bury the horses next to one another in the pasture. After that, Dad let the neighbor graze his cattle in there to keep the weeds down.

Around that time Dad would be retiring from the state. He retired at the age of 62, but not because he wanted to. I think he would have kept working, but modern technology was coming, and Dad would have to use a computer if he would have stayed any longer. There was no way that was going to happen. He said, "it was a bunch of happy horse shit." Whatever that meant. Either way he wasn't going to stick around to figure it out. So we gave him a retirement party. I had a video of his life in the navy, with my mom, and the life with Ruby and all of us kids. He cried every time he watched it. Tim asked me why I didn't let him know about it. Well, it was because it was from me. I didn't want him to know about it. Anyway, this left Dad with a lot of time on his hands. So he would always do his woodworking or help a neighbor out, or go running around and visit all the kids that lived out of state. He also acquired diabetes. This was part of the reason Dad couldn't see too well when he was driving. So he decided to start taking care of himself and went on a diet. He did really good taking his sugar count and giving himself injection in his big belly. He would always make a joke out of it. He would aim the needle at himself like he was going to commit Harry Carry. Then after sticking himself he would lunge forward and gasp a little. But I was proud of him because I know it was something he didn't want to do because he hated doctors and dentists.

After Dad retired, we started going turkey hunting together. So when spring gobbler season rolled around, Dad and I thought we would give it a shot. The first year we went out we went to a neighbor's field that had strips of trees that grew up and down the hillside. I thought I had seen a pair of turkey legs in one patch, so I told Dad to walk slowly up one side of the trees, and I would walk up the other side. I was hunched down low trying to see the turkey in the patch of trees. Trying to move slowly so I wouldn't spook them and make them fly off and I got to the top of this steep hill and there was Dad already! He didn't walk slowly at all, and was standing at the top of the hill, rolling a cigarette, and getting a kick out of my stalking technique. I thought to myself, what the heck is he doing up here already. Needless to say, I felt like a dummy. Then Dad decided he was going to sit in one spot and I was going to go get the turkey to come in to where I could get a shot. I thought I would go and scout out the wooded area outside of where we were hunting, and I'll be damned if I didn't get lost out there. I just kept on walking around getting a glimpse of that bird every now and then. Anyone who said turkeys are stupid had never come across this bird. He led me on a wild goose chase all over those woods. Being lost didn't help either. Eventually I listened for some cars on the road and started heading in that direction. I finally saw the road up ahead. But what road was it? I ended up walking across this guy's back yard all decked out in camo, packing a double barrel shotgun. He was working under the hood of his car out in his driveway. I unloaded the shotgun and apologized for trespassing and asked him where the hell I was. Apparently, I wound up some 2.5 miles in the other direction. I asked him if he could give me a ride back to where we were hunting. He obliged, and told me that he had gotten lost once, too. He took me back to where Dad was and I came walking up the hill. Dad was still sitting in the same place! I came up to him and told him what had happened to me. We took a ride down the road to where I had come out at and neither one of us could believe how far I had gone. After that I learned to not chase the turkeys.

The next morning we decided to hunt across the street. Dad's friend owned about 60 acres over there, where we went deer hunting. There's a gravel path that runs down through the property. We were on one side and Dad's friend, Dean, agreed to hunt on the other side. So we separated and I was using my turkey call to call a big tom up out of the gulley. Pretty soon Dad came over and saw me pointing my gun, but he didn't see anything. I hit my turkey call again, and the tom was about to pop up over the hill. Dad laid down on the ground behind me. I'm telling you this was a Kodak moment! I was going to get to shoot my first turkey and Dad was right there to see it and share in the excitement of the kill. Right when that turkey stuck his head up so we could see where he was, Dean came over on our side and was going to bushwhack my bird out from under me. I looked at Dad and said, "He's going to mess up my hunt." I was upset. I worked hard trying to get that bird up that close. I hit my turkey call to let Dean know that Dad and I were right there and that idiot stood straight up and there went my bird, off in the other direction. I was in tears. I told Dad that Dean had done that on purpose. Dad didn't think at that time Dean had purposely scared that bird away from me; so I couldn't get a shot. But later on, we found out that he had scared the bird out of a tree, and crossed over to where we were to get at shot at it. I realized that Dean wasn't going to let a girl out hunt him. His chauvinistic attitude would come shining through every turkey season. Later on Dad admitted that I was right, Dean did ruin my hunt on purpose. I didn't like Dean too much after that. The next time we would go turkey hunting we would make sure that Dean wasn't going to be around to spoil anything for us. A few days later Dad and I decided to go back across the street and give it our best shot. Since the birds weren't responding to any calls, we would just have to wander around and be in the right place at the right time. Dean was down below in the bottoms working in the fields with his tractor, so the coast was clear for Dad and I to have the whole place to our selves. We split up. Dad went to the right and I went to the left. Pretty soon I came along three jakes, (young toms). I had to be really cautious because a turkey's eyesight is as good as an eagles, and I didn't want them to flee. Armed with Dad's old double barrel shotgun, I waited it out, only moving when the birds were preoccupied with feeding. I was all camouflaged out, with face paint on, so I would blend into my surroundings. Dad always made fun of me, but I didn't care. It was going to be me or the bird. I managed to get into range, but there was a big patch of thorn bushes between the turkeys and me. There was only one small opening that I could look through to see them when they put their heads up. I aimed for the small opening through the bushes. Sure enough, one of those bird's heads was right there! So I shot it with the full choke barrel, "Bam!" I got the bird. The other two birds just stood there and were probably wondering what the heck was going on, since their buddy was flip-flopping around. But they soon fled the scene and I had to make my way over the barbed wire fence and around the thorn bushes to get to my bird. But when I finally got around there, I couldn't find my bird. He had flopped around and gone somewhere, but where? The area I shot him at was a hillside. Down below were the railroad tracks. So as I looked around, I heard flapping coming from below. I ran down to the tracks and there was my bird. I was so happy. I picked up the jake and started walking toward Dad on the railroad tracks. He saw me coming and had a big grin on his face. I got my first turkey! I couldn't wait to tell John. He was at work at the Highway Department. I took my bird out there to show him. We had our picture taken and it was put in the Highway Department newsletter. It was a proud moment and this time no one was there to spoil it for me.

After turkey season was over I got a phone call from Dad. When I answered the phone, he said, "Are ya home? I'll be right out." I said, "Okay." John asked who it was. I said, "It was Dad, I think he just poached something. He's bringing it right out!" So we prepared ourselves, knowing Dad it was hard telling what it was. Apparently Dad saw some turkeys down by the barn and made a bet with my brother Ross that he could shoot them. Ross said, "Not from this distance you're not going to get it." (Thinking that he was going to use a shotgun, which is what your supposed to use.) But Nooooo, Dad got the 308 deer rifle out and shot that bird and blew its freaking leg off. Ross was cussing, "Are you out of your mind, we're going to get busted." Dad said, "No we won't because you're going to go down there and get it." Dad shot that turkey well over 200 yards out. I guess because I got a turkey, he had to have one, too. When he brought it out to me, I went ahead and did a breast mount for him. He proudly displayed it upstairs with the rest of his trophies.

Soon Ross would be moving to a new location, only about five miles further down the road from Dad near the river on 179 Highway. It was a small house that had been a railroad depot at one time. So he could drive back and forth to work and would sometimes stop at Dad's, when he wasn't in the bars. He wouldn't have to travel that far when deer season rolled around. Tim and Ross would always meet at Dad's and they would all go over there together. I, on the other hand, was always already in my spot before sunrise. There was only one year that no one would see any deer, and that was because my stupid little brother, Tim, decided to go squirrel hunting the day before deer season and shagged all the deer out of the area. He saw six deer that day and didn't bring home any squirrel. It was no wonder we didn't see any deer. When Tim started walking in the woods, he made so much noise that you would have thought an elephant was in there. That's how I got most of my deer. He would scare them all up my way. So later on there was a fresh deer kill on the road and Dad and I went and got it. That was the only deer we got that year.

The following year Tim was complaining that he was always put in a spot where there weren't any deer. So we all swapped places I went and sat where Dad was, only out further. Dad sat where Tim was, down below, and Ross, (with his smoking and coughing), sat where I was. There was no reason why Tim couldn't get a deer, unless of course it was because he was a lousy hunter. He made too much noise, always propped his gun up on a tree, and stood there with his hands in his pockets. My gun was always in my hands ready to shoot. I ended up with an eight-point buck. Dad shot a seven-point buck down below where Tim always was. When we went to get Ross's truck to load up Dad's deer, Tim came down and was pissed off, (spoil sport). Dad and he got into it because Dad let Tim use the 45-70, (small cannon), and Tim threw it in the back of the truck bed. (We didn't know it at the time that the sights were knocked off because of how hard the gun hit the truck bed.) One thing Dad always taught us was to never abuse our guns! Of course after that Dad called Tim a few choice names. Tim stormed away telling Dad that he wished Dad was dead. I hated Tim for that comment, because he never had any respect for anyone anyway. I prayed that Tim would regret saying that to Dad come next deer season. Even though we didn't realize it that prayer was already answered. Because of the fit Tim had, even if he did get a bead on a deer, his sights were off on his gun and I didn't even care.

After things calmed down, Dad and I had a heart to heart talk. He stated that he didn't want Tim to have everything. That he didn't deserve certain things. That's when I told him about making out a will, because as spoiled as Ruby had made Tim, we all knew who would try to get everything. Tim was a hateful individual. He treated everyone like we were all in his way of getting everything he thought he should have. He never smiled in any of the pictures or videos. I remember I was taping a video at Christmas one year over at Dad's house. Tim wouldn't smile. I asked him, while the camera was on him to smile. He said he quit smiling in 1986. I asked, "What happened in '86?" He replied that's when Cassey, his daughter was born. I have that on videotape. I just said okay and turned the camera off of him.

Dad and Ruby found an attorney to make their wills out. There was a dispute about Ruby wanting Tim to be the main beneficiary. Dad didn't want it that way because he always tried to treat us all equally. So my sister

Molly was appointed as the personal representative, and those of us who lived here in Missouri would assist her. The will had certain things in it that Dad wanted certain kids to have and the rest was to be sold and divided up equally among us. To make sure his wishes were to be carried out, Dad gave some of us copies of the will, without Ruby knowing it. However, our copies were not notarized. The original will would be in a safety deposit box at the bank. With some of us having some peace of mind, life went on as usual.

Soon it was time for John and I to buy another feeder calf to raise for meat. Since the livestock barn was only open during the weekdays and John had to work, I decided to take Dad with me. He hadn't been to an auction barn in a long time. With the cattle racks on the back of our truck, Dad and I were on our way. There was a little restaurant inside the barn so we could grab a bite to eat if we got hungry. The place was completely air-conditioned. I went up to the teller and registered for a number. Dad got to see how things were done and had a good time. I would bid on the cattle coming in down in the arena. Dad would help me pick out a good one. I bought a heifer with one blind eye and one with its tail cut off. Dad and I didn't care because we didn't eat the eyeballs or tail anyway. Besides, these ones were cheaper. Farmers wouldn't buy any cattle with deformities. We were just looking at steaks and meat on the hoof. Before we loaded up our heifers, we made sure the vet on hand inoculated them. We loaded up and headed back to the house with our future delicacies. Dad and Ruby would always come out to see how the two calves were doing. Dad was looking forward to the next meat process party.

Since I had some free time from the taxidermy business, I was always going over to Dad's and we would always go somewhere or do something. Occasionally, Dad and Ruby would go to the Ponderosa restaurant, and of course, I never refused the offer of tagging along. They had a buffet with lots of fried chicken wings. If the place didn't have a buffet, then Dad wouldn't eat there. So every time we went in there the waitresses would always know what we would want. They knew us when we walked in there and Dad would always leave the girls a good tip. We would always fill our pockets with chicken wings, (wrapped up in a napkin of course), and the waitresses would always give Ruby a bag of shrimp because they knew that's what she liked. Then we would go riding around somewhere and go in some second hand stores. I remember looking at a mermaid trinket that I thought was cute, and Dad bought it for me when I wasn't looking. He gave it to me in the van when we left the store. It's in my main bathroom on a shelf of its own.

Through the years John and I always tried to pick out gifts that Ruby and Dad could use. Ross, on the other hand, would always go in with Tim and buy things like cap and ball rifles and stuff like that. I would never go in on anything that I thought Tim would inherit. John and I would buy them things to fix the house up with, because things were falling apart. Even though Dad could live with it, we couldn't. So every year they would get something for the house until Dad finally got the hint. One year we bought them a toilet because theirs would leak water all over the floor, and Dad would have to shut the valve off under the damn thing. So the only thing we could wrap was the toilet seat. Dad held it up and looked through it and smiled. Then when one of them had a birthday we all went in on some carpet for the living room because all the carpet in the house came from the capitol building. When they threw it out, then Dad would scarf it up. Next on the list was a stove for Ruby to cook on. The stove was dangerous and the oven always had to be lit with a match. It was probably the same stove that blew up in my face several years ago, back in the other house in Lowville. I was probably around fourteen years old at that time. I went downstairs to the kitchen one morning to turn the stove on. When it didn't' come on I stuck my head in the oven to light it, and it blew up in my face! I ran upstairs and told Carol that my face was on fire! I didn't have any eyebrows, nose hair, or eyelashes. I smelled like burned hair. My face was beet red and sore. If it was the same stove then it had to go. Dad finally took the hint and bought Ruby a new stove and a new couch. I would also buy him some lumber for our woodworking projects and for the plaques he made me for my taxidermy business, plus any tools he needed. But one gift we gave them that really stood out, was the pair of young turkeys dad named Tom and Tina. They were big white turkeys. Tom would always strut around us and show off. One day Tina died. We don't know what happened to her but Tom was sad for a long time and horny. He took an interest in Dad's blue jeans. Everywhere Dad went in the yard, Tom was there, struttin' and gobbling. Until one day, Dad had to work on his truck. He was bent over and I guess Tom just couldn't resist any more and started jumping on Dad and spurring him and trying to mount Dad! So every time Dad went out to work on the truck he would have to put a fence around him to keep the bird off of him. When he mowed the lawn Tom was always in the way, trying to turn on his new found love. Well, little did Tom know, Dad was counting the days. That year, the horny turkey was on our Thanksgiving table. He weighed around 40 pounds. No wonder Dad had such a hard time with him.

Dad was doing really well with his diabetes thus far. I was proud of him for taking care of it the way he was supposed to. He took his blood sugar regularly and was never without his medications. He knew better than to eat too many sweets. I would change my dessert recipes on holidays so he wouldn't get left out. I always took Dad into consideration, no matter what. One year Tim's wife, Jeana, made Dad and I some cookies and put them in coffee cups for Christmas gifts for us. I guess she thought I had a sugar issue, too. Neither Dad nor I could eat the damn things. Instead of using a diabetic recipe, she just eliminated half of the ingredients. They smelled like play dough and had the same consistency, too. Dad and I threw them away.

Well, it was going on another deer season and hopefully Tim stayed out of the woods before hand this time. I shot a small six point buck right off the get go. We would always sit until at least 11:00 AM, until every one had a chance to shoot something. After I shot my buck I just sat quietly for a while inside the cedar tree I used for shelter. I kept hearing something clicking behind me, and I knew better than to turn around because deer will try to get things to move if they're not sure what it is. It was really close and I had a feeling that something was staring at me. So I turned my head really slowly to look through the tree and there was a cute little doe with her head in my tree staring at me. I froze and we were face to face for a moment. I told her that it was her move because I was busted. Either turn around and go back into the woods, or come on out where I can shoot ya. She chose to go back into the woods and disappeared. Not long after that a shot rang out! It was the 45-70. Tim finally got to shoot something. So assuming he finally got to kill a deer we all quit, picked up my buck and waited for Tim. Well, he apparently wounded the doe. I chose to go with him to look for her, while Ross and Dad stayed behind with my buck. So little brother and I started following the bloody trail, and what a bloody trail it was. I didn't know what was keeping that deer going! As soon as we came across a spot where she had tried to bed down, I told Tim we would have to come back the next morning or that evening to get her so she could bed down and probably bleed out. But no, he wasn't going to listen to me. Since I knew that he wasn't going to be able to drag it out by himself, I stuck with him. That poor little doe tried to bed down three times. Stupid Tim just kept at her until she was way out of our jurisdiction. Finally, I gave up and left him go. If he'd have just listened then we would have had her that night. When I caught back up to Dad and Ross, who had been waiting patiently, I told them what Tim was doing. We all knew that the deer was going to wind up being coyote bait. It was a shame. After we took care of my deer Dad took the 45-70 and shot it. That's when we realized that the scope was off. Dad and I knew how it got that way, unfortunate for the deer. We didn't realize it at the time, but that was going to be our last hunt together.

The following spring I had taken a part time job working for the nuclear plant during their annual refueling that happened every 18 months. It was good money and was tough taking the course just to qualify. I had to go through the FBI and take a psychological test before they would even consider me, or anyone else working there. Then I had to go through a training course and pass several tests through a union training course. I worked 12 hours a day, seven days a week for four months straight, and never missed a day. They kept me on a bit longer for the last minute clean up. The taxidermy business was going okay, but I needed a steady job with benefits, so as I finished up some last minute customers, I decided to call it quits. It would have been all right if my customers would have come and picked up their mounts when they were ready, (even though I made them pay for half up front.) But there was always some excuse, and I would end up keeping stuff for months. Plus I had a freezer full of my own things that were in there for three years that I wanted to get to. There were coyotes, a blue indigo peacock, a 53-inch rattlesnake, and at least $3000 dollars worth of animals and birds that were already cleaned and packaged just waiting to be put together. There was also a pair of ornamental oriental pheasants that I was proud of that were ready to go. All I had to do was take something out and put it together, all the other work was done. I wanted to get to my own stuff, which left some of my customers very sad, and for years after that they would call the house and beg me to do their mounts. One guy offered to pay double. But eventually it had to go, times were changing.

Soon it was going to be Carol's birthday and Dad and I had to come up with something good to tell her. So we got her on the phone and Dad told her about a backhoe that we bought so we could go into our own landscaping business. She swallowed it, so I told her about running into the garage with it and everything. I told her that Dad was trying to teach me how to operate it. Then when she started getting worried that one of us was going to get hurt, we told her the truth. She didn't believe us! I guess we lied too good, and it took some time to convince her that we had just made it all up. I know what your thinking; how cruel. But she is an April Fool's baby, and we just had to have a little fun with her.

Dad and I passed on the spring turkey season that year. We decided it wasn't worth going out for. The spring rains were in full swing and we knew the season wasn't going to be a good one. Besides, Dean was probably down there anyway. I had all I could stand of him in the past. Things weren't going well in my marriage, either. Just like other marriages we were having some issues. I put my applications in elsewhere and got hired at a shop just outside of Jefferson City. John was having some issues where he was working, too. A divorce was inevitable. Since there weren't any kids involved, the attorney's fee was small. In the long run we parted as friends. We agreed that we were friends before we were married and would remain friends afterward. We didn't grab each other's stuff or take more than what we started with like most couples in a divorce. After getting an apartment in town and working for a while at my new job, John came over and told me that he had cancer. He was supposed to see a specialist in November for back surgery, but as I saw his condition rapidly deteriorating I called the doctor up and he was soon scheduled. I stuck by him to help him any way I could. He had to go to St. Louis for a bone marrow transplant. Even though I couldn't go with him, it was a long hard road to his recovery. At about that time it was time for me to buy a house. I found a nice ranch style house in Jefferson City. Dad liked it and could imagine all of my animals hanging on the tall ceilings. For a house gift, Dad bought me a gun safe and we put it in one of the closets. He gave me the 25-20 and the double barrel shotgun that I killed my turkey with. He knew that they were going to have a safe place now. We didn't tell anyone about the gun safe.

While John was going through his crisis, me buying a house, trying to learn new jobs at work because of a layoff they just had, and working on the night shift, Dad started gagging and having a hard time keeping his food down. I made an appointment with a specialist to check out Dad. He would have to go in for an endoscopy as an outpatient in the hospital. We all went to wait for him in the waiting room, (except Tim). We were left waiting a long time; Dad was getting impatient, and wanted to leave. He was saying how he could live with his gagging. I sat him back down and told him that we couldn't; he was going to get this taken care of, no matter what. I guess the doctor had an emergency and that's why we had to sit there a little longer. That was October 21, 1999. Dad was finally in and then was recovering to go home. He was to have another appointment on the 9th of December with the same doctor to discuss the results of his test. When that day came we went in with Dad to hear what was going on because we knew it was serious. Even Tim showed up later on. Anyway, the doctor told Dad that he had esophageal cancer. A cancerous lump was blocking his esophagus, and he would have two choices on how to take care of it. One way was with surgery and a small amount of chemotherapy, or radiation and chemotherapy. I wanted him to have the surgery, but Dad was always afraid that he would never wake up from that, so he went with radiation and chemo. After we were given the bad news and had a plan set for Dad's recovery, little brother showed up, and had to be filled in on what was happening. I couldn't believe how happy Tim was. He came out in the waiting room and told Ross, Richy and me that mom was going to give him power of attorney over all of their assets. I couldn't believe it, and I am not making this up. He had already planted Dad in the ground and was already making plans on everything he was going to get. When I got the chance I asked Ruby about it and she said that she never told Tim any such thing. He showed no emotion for Dad at all. So on December 2, 1999, Dad would have a port put in his chest so the chemo could be administered, and on the 6th he would have his first chemo treatment. His treatments were very aggressive. Every week I took him in to the cancer hospital and he would be there from about 9:30 AM until around 3:30 PM. He would always be sick for a few days afterward and by the time he would feel well, it would be time for another round. Since I hadn't had my house for long, I still had some unpacking to do, too. While Dad was in having chemo, I would always take Ruby out shopping and we would pick up any groceries or anything they needed. Dad was going to need pain medications that I would always pick up for him. The doctors explained how Dad couldn't be around people with colds or that were sick because his immune system was down because of the chemo. It was hard for the grandkids, (Tim's), to understand this. His kids' noses were always runny and I would just cringe when they were over to Dad's. Plus Dad wouldn't stop going out on the front porch in his bare feet to get wood for the wood stove. After two plus months of harsh chemo, Dad came down with pneumonia and I took him to the hospital. He was just way too sick for it to have been just from the chemo. The doctor stopped the chemo and after Dad got out of the hospital he had to start the radiation therapy, which went pretty good. The cancer was nearly gone anyway. While Dad was in Chemo therapy John, too, was in there getting his chemo at the same time, so they would both spend time together in the hospital getting chemo. After that I was taking Dad to radiation. His treatments were about an hour long. He would show everyone the map that was drawn on his belly for the coordination numbers that the radiation machine had to use to zero in on his cancer. After several of those treatments Dad would be feeling a lot better and we could rest a little better. It was long into the summer before those treatments were finally over. Dad had also quit smoking at that time too, and had talked Ruby into quitting. I don't think he would have stopped, but the chemo he was on made him sicker when he tried to smoke. It was going to be awhile before he could get his diabetes back in check. For the most part Dad was doing all right. The cancer left him weak and I was over at the house helping him with whatever Ruby and he needed. He seemed like he changed some. Every time I would pick Ruby up to go shopping, he would always tell her to spend whatever she wanted and buy whatever she wanted. So she and I would always make a day of it and bring Dad something home to eat. I took them both to the doctors, grocery shopping and wherever they needed to go. I was the only one they could count on.

Since my divorce, I had a big freezer that Dad and I moved into Ross's house. I had to rent an apartment until my house was ready to move into. It had needed some work done before I could move into it. Ross would keep my taxidermy freezer with all my prized possessions in it, for me in the meantime. I didn't want it over at Ross's. He couldn't keep his mouth shut, and he was a compulsive liar. So that was a really good reason to get it to my house as soon as possible. But every time Dad and I tried to get a hold of Ross; he would always blow us off. I wanted my freezer home, and so did Dad. I had over $3,000 worth of already prepped animals in that freezer. I was going to do a wall mount with the peacock and put it on my wall. I was already making preparations on what and where they were going to go. But we couldn't get a hold of Ross. He would work and go straight to the bar. So one day Dad and I went down there, and I went in to try to talk to him about getting my freezer. But he was being a drunken smart aleck, so we left. Dad said that he would go over there in person to his house, (since Ross just lived up the road from Dad), and talk to him about it. After four weeks of Ross avoiding Dad and I, Dad called me up and said that Ross sold his house and that my freezer was thrown out into someone's cow pasture. I rushed over to Dad's and we went to Ross's house. And some people were in there tearing out the carpet. I couldn't believe the condition that the house was in. The concrete steps at the front door had a terrible urine smell from Ross urinating out the front door. The bathroom was awful. The tiles were all off the wall, and the shower was completely wrecked. The living room had beer cans all over the back of the couch and beer cans were stacked everywhere. Ross never told us that he was selling the house and that his neighbor wanted it for his daughter. He told Dad that the freezer went out. Well, it didn't go out. He had his electricity shut off. For a month Dad and I tried to get a hold of him. Dad and I drove out to where my freezer was and when we looked in it, I was shocked, over half of my stuff was missing! The peacock, my ornamental pheasants and my snake were all gone. All that hard work skinning, de-fatting and fleshing, and washing; was all down the tubes. And what happened to the rest of my stuff? Gone . . . I wanted to kill Ross. I was ready to go to that bar and drag his stinkin' ass out of there and beat the holy crap out of him. I was crying and upset, and Dad calmed me down and told me that Ross couldn't help it; that he had an illness. I wanted to give him a black eye and a few broken ribs to go along with his illness. Ross avoided Dad and I like the plague for a long time after that. My freezer was buried in the pasture and I didn't care to talk to Ross after that.

Since Dad's illness was stabilizing and John was back home and recovering from his ordeal with cancer, I could now start concentrating on things I needed. I worked a lot of overtime and met new people. I started seeing someone that was going through a rough time himself. We would always get together and talk. His name is Eddie and he also worked at the same shop I did. We got along pretty good for the most part, and Dad thought he was a nice guy. On the weekends I would often help Eddie out on some property he had, 28 miles out of Jefferson City. He had a building that he would have sound systems for the kids to dance and party at. Whatever the kids tore up we would put back together. He also had a fishing pond that I could never catch anything but tiny perch out of. John started working for his brother after his recovery. He was also adopting an abused German Shepherd, and raising a pup of his own. He seemed to be bouncing back pretty good. This was the first year that we wouldn't be going out deer hunting. If Dad didn't feel very good, then none of us would go out. Ross and Tim said they only went out because Dad wanted to, but I wanted to go because I liked it. We didn't go deer hunting in the year 2000. This allowed Dad to recover more. I was concerned about him catching pneumonia again, anyway. I helped Dad run the log splitter and filled the front porch up with wood, so that would be all taken care of for him and Ruby.

When the year 2001 rolled around, Dad's hair was all grown back, and he decided to grow a beard. His hair grew back better after the chemo treatments. His beard was thicker than before and his bald spot was covered with hair. Since he had lost some weight, his diabetes was under control and he didn't need to inject himself as often. Ruby would always get onto him about not taking his insulin shots, but he didn't need to. For the most part everything seemed to be going okay. I still took Ruby and Dad everywhere they needed to go. In the meantime Dad's teeth were looking pretty bad. Years of doing his own dentistry, was catching up with him. He decided to go to a dentist and inquire about some dentures. Ruby, Dad and I went to the Lake, where they were advertising dentures for $250. Since she needed her dentures relined, we were hoping to kill two birds with one stone. We went and we waited. Dad's took longer because he had some teeth that had to be dug out and surgically removed, (because he filed them down to a nub). Ruby's were another story. Her gums had shrunk up so much that we wasn't sure there was anything that could be done. Dad got to keep some of his lower teeth, so he just had to have an upper done. When we left Ruby had her dentures relined but was told to not soak them, like she did the old ones. She soaked them anyway and within six months, I was taking her back. Dad and I went back to get his dentures since they were done, and when he put them in his mouth and gave a great big grin, I about died laughing. He was looking at himself in the mirror complaining that it felt like he had a mouthful of shit! I must say that all the years that I knew my dad, I had never seen him with so many teeth before. Of course he wasn't going to use any Polygrip either, which made matters worse. So his teeth wound up getting tossed aside and personally I didn't blame him. But that didn't stop us from going out and eating though.

He often would go out in his workshop and make some stuff for Ruby and I. He would get patterns and make us wheelbarrows, little carts, and flower containers. There was plenty of wood left over from when I had the taxidermy business, so he was set to go. Once in a while he would come over to my new house and check things out.

Around October that year, Dad's symptoms started coming back. I wanted him to go in and get it taken care of right away. But as usual, he wanted to wait until after the holidays. I told him that it was a fast growing cancer and waiting might not be such a good idea. He argued that he wanted to be able to eat during holidays. I told him that he was barely eating now, but it fell on deaf ears. That year for Thanksgiving Rosella and her husband John came down to visit. Everyone was at the kitchen table except Dad and John. As soon as we started eating John ran in the dining area and said that Dad was getting sick. Since no one else was going to go in there, (for fear of losing their appetite), I got up and took Dad a trashcan to gag in, got him a cold washrag and some water. He was in bad shape and I hated to see him suffer like that. After he was doing better, I took my plate in the living room and stayed in there with him to make sure he was going to be okay. He needed to know that we weren't going to bail out on him just because he was having a hard time keeping his food down. It was the 21st of February 2002. He would agree to go see the doctor. I made an appointment to a different doctor because the one he had before had moved. On the 25th Dad was in doing chemo again. This doctor didn't take as much of an aggressive course as the other one did. But Dad just had to go more often, and it didn't leave him feeling as sick as before. Since he was going through this again, I was often worried about how much strength he was going to have. The first time the chemo knocked him for a loop. The more he went the sicker he got. Every time I went to see him he was in the bedroom with the door shut, trying to yell for Ruby to help him. He either needed his bucket emptied or was starving. Ruby would turn her hearing aid off, the TV would be blasting, and she would be sitting there in the living room reading a book. I don't know what she was thinking, but Dad was in the bedroom wanting to die, because she wasn't there for him. It was torturous for him. When I asked her what she was giving him, all she was doing was putting a bullion cube in water and giving it to him. Well, that was dehydrating him because it was too salty and had no nutritional value. So I started making him some soup. She had all day to make him something, but all she would do was the bullion cube. I asked her how come she didn't cook him up some beef broth or chicken broth. She was more concerned about what to do with the left over cooked meat than she was my dad. I told her that Dad was worth more than a $3 chicken. She laughed at me. The next time I had to take Dad to the cancer doctor, I told him what she was giving Dad and asked him to tell her to stop giving him that crap, and he did. But it didn't stop her, so I went through the cupboards and took every bit of that stuff out, and threw it away. So I bought a small grinder, like she had, and started feeding Dad myself. I was so disgusted with her. She was just acting too lazy for me to deal with. So I cooked the chicken and beef and ran them through the grinder and bought some little tiny pebbly noodles and made Dad some soup that he could just drink down. He ate the heck out of it and was starting to regain some of his strength. I will be darned if Ruby wasn't eating the soup, too. She could eat anything she wanted, he couldn't. I was not a happy camper with her, but I had to bite my tongue, and do everything I could for the both of them.

At this time I realized that I needed to take some time off work. I wasn't getting any sleep. I was still on the night shift and they told me that I could take a FLMA, (Family Medical Leave of Absence). All I would need was a doctor's excuse from Dad's doctor. I didn't get paid though, but that was okay. So I was in and out of work all the time. Since Dad was on smaller doses of chemo, his treatments would be shorter but they would continue for several months. Eventually, he was back to driving around. Although he was still a little weak, he was getting around okay. Even though he didn't have any hair left, he still managed to have a moustache.

At around May Dad was doing pretty darn good, considering all that he had gone through. He didn't have to have the chemo as often and had his port taken out. A port is a tube that runs straight down into the main artery. The top is under the skin and bulges out so when a person is administered chemo, then the nurse can just hook the IV into the lump, (or bubble), at the top. Dad's was in his chest and the chemo IV would literally have a hook on it just for that purpose.

In the middle of June Dad would be getting a visit from his sister. She flew down to visit him when she found out he was having a tough time with cancer. They hadn't talked in over 39 years. She was one of the sisters that chose to not speak to my Dad when he married Ruby. I guess maybe she needed to ease her conscience, I don't know. But Dad was glad to see her. I was glad she came down, too. She stayed for a week and had a good time seeing Missouri. Dad was still a little weak, but he managed to bring her out to see my house. We all had a nice visit. I believe they were trying to make up for lost time. All was forgiven for any difference they had between them.

When Dad's birthday rolled around I wanted to take him fishing. Since I hadn't been successful catching anything in Eddie's pond, I didn't want to go there. I wanted Dad to have a good time catching fish. Dad wanted to go there anyway. We went and he drove us out there. At this time I noticed Dad was starting to get a little wobbly. I didn't think too much of it since he had been through a lot. We fished but I caught nothing, as usual. Dad caught two huge catfish. I did everything he did, used the same bait, fished in the same spot and still caught nothing. But he did. I was so happy that he had finally got to catch bigger fish than I did. I really didn't think either one of us was going to pull anything out since the pond was pretty much fished out by the previous owner. I thanked God for giving us such a good day. We took the fish back to the house and I took a picture of Dad and his big catch. He shared the fish with Eddie and I, and they were good.

Dad's wobbling was getting worse all the time. We dug out a walker for him that he had before. We were really puzzled as to what was causing this. On the 16th of July 2002, I took Dad back to the cancer doctor. No one knew what was going on, so he was admitted back into the hospital for some tests right away. He went with no fuss, while they spent days trying to figure out what the problem was. At first the doctor thought that the cancer had gone to his brain. After taking a CT scan and other tests, it all came back negative. We were grasping at straws trying to figure out what happened. Dad's health was progressively getting worse. I stayed with Dad at the hospital as much as I could. Dad told me about his Navy days and how he was a hero. This was something Dad never spoke about. He told me, "I guess I waited too long," referring to the holiday issue. All I could do was comfort him. One day he just quit talking. I was staying with him in the morning and the afternoons to make sure he had food and was able to eat. I wanted Ruby to stay in there with him one afternoon, so when he woke up, she would be there to keep him company. It was about 2:30 in the afternoon and Tim could take her home when he got off work. You would have thought I asked her to jump off a cliff; she started to panic and just couldn't handle staying there to keep him company. Tim was getting off work at 4:00, so it wasn't like she was being dumped off and abandoned. Tim wasn't any help either. He would pop his head in and say, "I'm not coming out here just to watch him sleep." So there was no comfort for Dad there. I wanted him to swing by there and just make sure Dad was getting a supper that he could eat. But of course, he didn't. He was too busy making other plans. After talking to Carol about what was going on, we talked about a neck injury Dad had a long time ago. So the neurologist was called in. In the meantime Dad had to be fed like a baby. He sat up in bed with a blank look on his face. Although he wasn't talking he could communicate with his eyes. He would play games with his eyes. But he would have to be told what to do, like sucking on a straw, looking in his mouth to make sure he chewed up all his food before getting another bite. When I told Eddie about the condition Dad was in, he couldn't believe it and came to the hospital with me one day. The following Monday the neurologist came in and took some tests on Dad. The next morning I was there when he came in to tell Dad what he had found. Dad's neck had arthritis in it, and some bone had slivered off and was cutting into his spinal cord. I remember him bending over my dad in the hospital bed and telling him he was sorry. All they could do was to keep him calm and comfortable. At this time there still wasn't anything mentioned about whether or not he was dying. Either way,

I wasn't going to give up hope because he was still communicating with us. He would let me know if he needed rubbed or covered up. One morning I picked Ruby up, and Ross, she and I went to hospital. Dad was in a terrible state. They had him in bed with a diaper on and he was thrashing around. The nurse told me that they took him in for another endoscopy. A person's neck has to be tilted back in order to get the scope down the throat. Since Dad's spinal cord was already damaged, I believe it caused more damage. We didn't know if he was having a hard time coming out of anesthesia or what. When it went on for hours we knew something was definitely wrong. I asked the nurse if there wasn't something that could be done for him and that's when she told me that I should contact the family. All the time Dad was thrashing around he would look at me and grab my hand and try to pull me down toward him, as if to say, "save me." There was nothing I could do for him. He didn't grab at anyone else, just me. I knew he was trying to tell me something, but all anyone could do was keep talking to him, and try to get him to calm down. We stayed all day and half the night before he was finally taken into a private room. Some time in the night he slipped into a coma. Once again Tim never showed up. That was on a Thursday. After contacting everyone I went back to the hospital. I didn't want Dad to be alone, but I was exhausted. Rich and Ellen stayed that night with Dad, so I could try and get some rest. Aunt Punk was coming into the St. Louis airport, and since Tim wasn't doing anything, we made him go pick her up and bring her to the hospital. So Rich, Ellen, Aunt Punk and I stayed the night with Dad Friday night. Dad's eyes were open all this time, so to prevent them from drying out, I took a warm washcloth and told Dad that he had to keep his eyes closed, and I closed his eyes and held them shut with the washcloth for a couple of minutes and he kept them closed the whole time, after that. He would have seizures and every time he had one, his blood pressure would drop. But we could continue talking to him all the time because we were always told that a person's hearing was the last to go. We didn't ever want Dad to think that he was by himself, so we tried to concentrate on all the fun things we did with him. I always told him how proud I was of him the whole time. When Saturday rolled around, Eddie and I made a dash to the St. Louis Airport to pick up Carol. I think I drove 80 mph all the way there. Some of the other family members were slowly coming in from other states. So Carol, Aunt Punk and I stayed with Dad that night. When Sunday rolled around, everyone was at the hospital. Even my cousins Rich and Bob, (who were Dad's favorite nephews), were on their way from New York and Pennsylvania, trying to get there in time.

I kept telling Dad to hang in there because I knew he would want to hear their voices one last time. After taking a few wrong turns, they finally got there. I told them each to take Dad's hands and tell him that they were there and that they loved him. As if it was what he was waiting for, Dad calmly took his last breath. I announced that Dad was gone and Aunt Punk started singing an old gospel tune that was always a favorite of Dad's. I was glad she was there. We all got to go in one last time to be alone with Dad to say our special goodbyes. Ruby didn't seem to understand what was going on. She was all smiles when we were all standing around the hospital bed, like we were having a reunion. After Dad was gone my sisters took her into the restroom and apparently had to explain to her what had just happened and that's when she collapsed. I don't know what she thought was going on.

After that we all had to go to the funeral home and make arrangements. Dad was cremated and his visitation cost a whopping $2,800 total. His ashes would be sent to the navy for a burial at sea. He wanted his ashes to be at the bottom of the north Atlantic. It was the least that Tim could do, so he made the arrangements.

When Dad passed away, it was the beginning of the end for our family unit. Dad kept us all together as a family, and Ruby wasted no time letting us know who she was putting in charge. No matter who tried to help her, it was going to be what Tim wanted and that was pretty much that. So with Tim in charge everything went to hell. Dad's truck was put up for sale. It was only worth about $700 but Tim wanted over $1,000. Even though Ross and I knew people who was interested in buying it for over $600, Tim wasn't going to let it go. So Dad's truck sat out there and rotted until Tim could only get $200 for it. Then he started buying all kinds of things. He had bad credit and couldn't even get a loan before. But some how he came up with enough money to buy an used RV, a Bronco, (full-sized, used) and brand new living room furniture for his house. The money wasn't coming from Ruby's bank account, because I kept an eye on that. The only other place he would have gotten it was from all the savings bonds Dad collected through the years. Dad always told me when he bought another bond. Dad collected savings bonds for 20 years after we moved here. When Molly, Ruby and I, (I don't know who else was with us), went to the bank and got into the safety deposit box to get Dad's will there was a fistful of savings bonds. Molly picked them up and was impressed by how many there was. After Dad passed away and every one had gone, Carol stayed behind to help Ruby adjust to being alone, and to try to help her get some things done. But she wouldn't let Carol do anything, not even paint the bedroom. Only

Tim could make these decisions. I don't think there was any appreciation coming from Ruby, especially since Carol left her own family to stay down here and help her out. It didn't matter what anyone did for Ruby because Tim was going to have the last say, except when it came to the guns that my dad wanted certain kids to have. He wanted me to have the 357 magnum and the K-22 pistols. I was going to make sure I got them, but Tim wanted all the guns for himself. I took the both of them to Dad's attorney and I not only got my pistols, but Molly got her two 22 caliber rifles and Carol got Dad's old 38 revolver that was in our family for over 50 years.

But after Ruby lied to me for four years telling me that she would never change the will; that she would never do that to our Dad or us kids, she did. She did it less than two years after Dad's passing and gave the house, land and everything to Tim. No wonder two years after Dad died Tim wanted to put central air, new washer and dryer and everything in the house. He wanted it fixed up for him. Ruby didn't need central air, there were two window air units in the house that she wouldn't even use. She was cold all of the time. By the time he got done making all these unnecessary improvements, nearly all of the savings bonds would be gone. When Ruby needed to go to the doctors or grocery store, or just wanted to get out for a while, I would take her. She never had to stay home.

But one day Molly called and wanted Ruby to come down to Louisiana to visit with her for a while. I told Molly that Ruby had dementia and when she was in strange places her mind would go blank. Well Molly assured Ross, Rich, Tim and I that she knew all about that, since her husband had just passed away, and he was an elderly gentleman. So we let Ruby go. There were three deaths in the family within a year's time. John, who was Rosella's husband, died from throat cancer in September 2002, and Molly's husband, Ed, died the following year in May, and of course, Dad.

Since Mom was with Molly, I needed to go by the house and pick something up. Since Ross was supposed to be keeping an eye on things and feeding the dog, I asked him to meet Eddie and I out there. That's when he confessed about Dad's neck injury. He told me Tim and he were supposed to help Dad out of the bathtub. Dad got a hold of the both of them and Tim never showed up. I don't know why they didn't get on the phone and call Tim, but they didn't. So Ross was the only one to help Dad get out of the tub. Plus we converted the bathtub into a shower. I don't know what anyone was thinking. When Dad was ready to get out of the tub, Ross would be the only one there to help him out, and Ross was a total weakling. So as he tried to pick Dad up, Dad slipped and fell backwards hitting the back of his neck on the tub. This news just blew me away. All that time we spent in the hospital trying to figure out what was going on with Dad, Ross knew all along and never said a word. Now I know that we are supposed to love one another and all that; but there were two people in this family that were really making me mad, and that was Tim and Ross. Once again I felt the need to strangle him, (Ross), and didn't care if he drank himself to death after that.

Anyway, while Molly had Mom she took her to Alabama to introduce her to her fiancée. Mom wound up getting lost in the house looking for the bathroom and fell down the stairs. Molly didn't let anyone know what happened. Ruby wound up with several bruises on her and her head took a jostle and her brain swelled up. It was a serious issue. After Ruby healed up enough and underwent rehab, Tim flew down to Alabama and brought Ruby back and put her in a nursing home. Tim told the nursing home superintendent that Ruby's house was worth $125,000, so the nursing home made Tim appraise the house and land and told him that Ruby couldn't stay there because she didn't have enough equity. Her house was only worth about $60,000 and he would have to move her. So he found the cheapest place to put her. I know because my friend worked there and would have to feed Ruby sometimes; and she told me, that usually that was a place where they put people with no money. The state took care of most of the people there. They put her in the same ward as the Alzheimer's patients, which I thought was a mistake. She didn't have Alzheimer's. When I would go and see her, she was fragile and the others were fit as a fiddle and would run around every evening trying to get the doors open. Her glasses were always gone and her hearing aid would disappear. And I really thought that Tim loved his mom enough to do the very best for her. But she ended up getting run over by these crazed Alzheimer patients and wound up with a broken hip. I was there when she came out of surgery and she seemed to be doing all right. She was losing her strength and started to dehydrate after having to go back to the nursing home. My friend kept telling me that Ruby needed to be moved out of there and I kept passing the message on to Tim. But it fell on deaf ears. No wonder, he never went to visit his own mom while she was there. Only when someone came in from somewhere else, would he go see her. My friend showed me Ruby's chart where people had to sign in before they could visit anyone and his name was only on it once a week. He didn't care. He was making plans to move into his new home that he inherited. While Ruby's tongue was all shriveled up and she was staring to curl up from dehydration, Tim finally got up off his ass and had her sent to the hospital. They got fluids into her and she started looking better. But she was dying. Ross spent most of the time in the hospital with her. When I asked him if he had seen Tim, the answer was always, "I haven't seen him." After Ruby passed away, some of us seemed to have a difference of opinion on how much to spend on her cemetery marker. Rosella, who had more money that the rest of us because John won the lottery, seemed to think that we should all pitch in $100 a piece. Well, some of us couldn't afford that much and besides, no one cared that Dad didn't have a marker.

We didn't have anywhere to pay our respects to Dad. So Carol and I went in on a marker for him. The Navy supplied the bronze plaque. We all decided that $45 from each of us was what were all going to pitch in for Ruby's marker. There were nine of us kids. It was a nice marker with all our names on it. So Tim had Ruby buried out in the middle of what used to be a cow pasture fifteen miles out of Jefferson City, which was the cheapest place he could find. He could have put her right next to Dad's marker, but he didn't. The last time I went out to see her grave, the weeds were 12 inches tall, and I got bug bit just trying to get to it. Unfortunately, not too many people go out to pay their respects there. No one seemed interested in seeing Dad's marker. Rich and Ellen and I are the only ones who visit Dad's marker. But that's okay, it gave some of us some closure. It makes me happy to see his name in the veteran's section and I can have a place to go and take him flowers on special occasions.

Anyway, Tim and Jeana pretty much cleared out all of the valuable stuff out of the house first and left the things they didn't want to the rest of us. All but $2,200 of Dad's savings bonds were spent, and Ruby wanted Carol and I to have those. We were grateful. We all got a share of what was left over from the bank account. All the clothes I bought Ruby were already given to one of Tim's kids to cut up to wear. Some of those dresses cost $50, and were going to be cut up to fit a nine year old. All of Ruby's jewelry that I bought her was gone. (They were all gemstones.) It was obvious that everything had been picked through. My little brother had two choices. He could have either kept us all together as a family and divide everything up equally like Dad wanted, which including selling the house, or he could be greedy and throw us all under the bus. He chose to throw us all under the bus.

Ross and Rosella are the only two that keep in touch with Tim. The rest of us keep in touch with each other with phone calls, since we all live in different states. But life goes on and we all have to find a way to live with what life hands us, no matter how good or bad, or happy or sad. I miss my dad every day. There's a constant reminder of who he was and what kind of man he was in every room of my house.

But most of all, I just wanted the people who never got to know him, to have a piece of history of who this man was, and what he tried to do for everyone. All the time he was alive, all we thought about was his heart and if it would hold out, since he had all those heart attacks in the past. His heart was strong throughout everything he had to go through. It was the last to go. So I guess I just wanted to give a testimony for my dad. Maybe when I get to be 70 or 80 years old, and I start to forget some things, I can go back, read, and remember again who my dad was, remember some of the crazy things he did, remember the good times he shared with us growing up, and have a laugh or two.

Written by
Karen Jean (Brown) Benne
February 1, 2010

Dad's favorites

Color: Blue
Flower: Dahlias
Holiday: Thanksgiving
Sayings: "Go hammer your ass", "Ain't that a bunch of happy horse shit."
Things to do: Anything out of doors
             Helping others
             Woodworking
             Eating
Cars: Mostly the Model A's and Model T's or anything before 1960

In conclusion, I would just like to add a few more things. My dad, Theodore Robert Brown, wasn't afraid of anything. He was a risk taker and was always wanting to get involved. He would dive off a ship to save his friends from the frozen waters of the North Atlantic. He would hitchhike to work in all kinds of weather to support his family, when the car wouldn't start. He was a volunteer fireman. He was a Rent-a-Cop that went wherever he was needed. He would walk on the frozen water to rescue a goose in French Creek, and fell through the ice, knowing he would catch pneumonia, (and did). He was our hero. The good times and the fun we had with him will always out weigh the bad times. I thank our beloved Lord for giving us such a unique individual for a dad. He will always be remembered and loved.

A Poem. About "My dad"

He was a builder, a hunter, an adventurer, and a teacher;
A law enforcer, a lawbreaker, a rancher, and a preacher.

He would tease and aggravate, and be clever, and fun;
And he'd work along side of us, till the job was done.

He was six foot two, fearless and strong;
And he'd put the fear of God in us, whenever we did wrong.

And there were times, when we thought he was nuts;
But he raised all us kids, and that took some guts.

He was a doer, a worker, and a "take charge" kinda Dad;
Who provided us with every thing that we ever had.

And when my memory fails, and I start to feel sad;
Then I can look back and read, about all those times we had.

And although things are different now, I'll still get by;
Because we had a Dad who loved and cared about us, and that's
            "No lie."

www.ingramcontent.com/pod-product-compliance
Lightning Source LLC
Chambersburg PA
CBHW030407290526
45785CB00004B/1931